The Philosophy According To Thomas III:
The Holistic Warrior

By

Thomas J. Nolan III, Ph.D.
theholisticwarrior.com

ISBN
0-6156696-5-4 (10 digit)
978-06156696-5-6 (13 digit)

www.theholisticwarrior.com

Table of Contents

Expect Nothing;
Be Prepared For Anything:
The Mantra Of The Samurai Warrior

Dedication

This book has been dedicated to you, my daughters and grandchildren as well as my brothers and sisters, their children and grandchildren, the offspring of Thomas and Evie Nolan. I want to give them a glimpse of how I have become the person I am and describe to them the process it took to get me to this point. I never thought of my life as being special or that interesting. However, as I have put together both past and current writings in this book, I am beginning to see the value of my unique experiences. I share these experiences and subsequent understandings with the reader in hopes of helping you bring order and understanding to your own unique set of experiences.

Acknowledgements

There have been many individuals who have made an impact on my thoughts, actions, and feelings. They helped me to better understand myself, how I fit into the world, and how to get where I wanted to go. So, I would like to thank and acknowledge those who have had a myriad of influences toward the writing of this book.

First, my wife of 32 years, Cecelia, she stands by and supports me, allowing me to "be me." Next, my daughters, Michelle and Nikki; who very early in their teenage years taught me the value of connecting and communication. Then, my oldest sister, Alice; we have travel this life as allies since I was one and a half; we have always supported and been there for each other.

Next, I'd like to recognize Dr. Pat Hart, decreased, who as my first major professor helped me to make sense and bring out my ideas that led to develop the foundation of my philosophy. At first, I resisted his input, so, it took me a while to realize that he was trying to help me. He helped me to find the additional data that supported my ideas, as well as, organize these ideas into a coherent structure.

I would also like to recognize my first two spiritual friends, Leslie (Jackson) Heslip and Levi Moten. Both of them helped me to understand that there were realities other than a scientific world, such as, the importance of intuition. They were probably the first people to know the multiple sides of me, the intellectual, the intuitive, and the sensitive, to name a few. They challenged me on all these levels and helped me to better understand myself. The first people I allowed to look at me critically, giving me welcome feedback about my thoughts, feelings, and actions.

Next, I would like to thank the many friends I have made within the metaphysical community. Here, I found a home, creating southern, northern, and western family groups. If anyone had told me I would be a practicing psychic, I would have laughed and called them crazy. These groups accepted me and helped me to accept the spirituals gifts I didn't initially know I had. With their encouragement, I was able to find a place for me by creating a reality that utilized both sides of the brain. Previously groups had always told me what I couldn't do even though I was doing it at the time, i.e., major in physics and minor in music, teach both psychology and chemistry courses, among many.

And, then, there are my friends, Paul and Alysn. We had a twelve year journey together, where we discussed and explored ideas from sacred geometry to alien conspiracies to spiritual development. We explored Colorado, including the western range of the Rocky Mountains, the hot springs in Glenwood Springs, mystical waterfalls along highway 133 to Marble, panning for gold near Golden, or hunting for treasure near the Sleeping Indian Mountain west of Castle Rock. It was one of the most productive and creative periods I have experienced, helping me to progress physically, mentally, emotionally, and spiritually.

There is also a group of people who provided special assistance with ideas, health information, and related areas, including Debbie Martin and Teri Ingle, Susan Jennings, Dashma Dovchin, Dennis Smith, Coyote and Elizabeth Prosapio, Josephine Flowers-Salehar, Yoni Brewer, and Rick and Emma Ferguson, among others. Discussions with these people have been very helpful and inspiring. A special recognition goes to Nancy Byers who also helped me to grow spiritually and introduced me a series of spiritual teachers and ideas that I would not have found on my own.

There is another group that has assisted me in gaining a better understanding of how we balance our energy. This group includes Cindy Smith who works with a Mayan Crystal Skull, named Osh and Rick Ferguson who has developed a chair called the Osiris Energy Chair. Meditations with Osh and in the Osiris Chair led to the development of the Aura photos shown on page 199 (the Six-Pointed Star over my heart, as well as, the clear geometric Chakras). This was the first visual evidence of the significance of my energy field in more than 25 years of taken aura photo.

And lastly, a group of people who proof read or gave me feedback about the readability of this book. This group includes Brenda Gillen and Mitchell Whittington who not only proofread the book but helped me to format the book as well. Then there is a group that proofread the book for readability, including Coyote Prosapio, Leslie Heslip, Santi, Terri Ingle, Rick Ferguson, Carol Brown, Cecelia Yoder, and, Rita Louise. A special thanks to Rick Ferguson who helped get my images and pictures in proper shape.

Purpose of This Book

I've lived more than 73 years and, as a result, have had a plethora of unique experiences that were both challenging and exciting. These experiences were unique not just because of the events themselves but because of the choices I made as well as the understandings I gained from the choices. At first glance, my choices did not always seem to be in my best interest. Many times they were skewed by my emotional and mental state of mind that drove or caused me to see life in terms of how these events hurt me. That is, decisions were made that were based on the pain I chose to feel at the time. Because these decisions led to consequences I didn't anticipate or like, I now seek to live life differently. At least now I see life in terms of how the events I experienced helped me, instead of hurting me. I accomplish this by choosing to work through the pain resulting from my perception of these events to prevent this pain from incapacitating me.

As a result of this approach, I have evolved a set of ideas about life, liberty and the pursuit of happiness. The purpose of this book has been to present these ideas. To make sense of the lifestyle that has evolved from these ideas, I've included many of the events and resulting experiences that led to their development.

There are at least two approaches one can take delineating their ideas. One, a formal approach where you show the historical and developmental work that leads to an expression of these ideas. And two, an operational approach where you express your ideas as stories and working principles that more completely allows the reader to identify with the results you came up with. In this presentation, I have used the second approach. I am also writing a second book that utilizes the first approach. It puts forward a complete derivation of my ideas and seeks to document them as well.

I have tried to give the reader a working knowledge of my approach to life as well as the evolutionary process it took me to reach this point. Much of this information is very personal. It also reveals my impressions of events and I understand the possibility and probability that it didn't happen according to my impressions or recollections. I'm sure that other people who experienced these events along with me will have an entirely different viewpoint. I realize that these events probably did not happen the way either of us remembers. So, more likely, there's my viewpoint, their viewpoint, and the way it really happened.

My understanding of the possibility of different viable viewpoints has become more and more apparent to me as I've gotten older. This process is especially true when you or I get caught up in the emotions of an event. And when you do, it is very hard to even sense that there are other possibilities, let alone other points of view.

These different points of view exist because we are all trying to get our needs met and we have vastly different ways of meeting these needs. Many, perhaps most, of the ways we use to achieve what we want are dysfunctional. It is this dysfunctional mind-set that caused me to view the events of life in terms of "they hurt me" instead of how these same events could help me. Dysfunctional behaviors are also supported by a pervasive undercurrent subsystem that affects all peoples of our culture or society.

Our culture and most cultures on this planet are supported by a system based on fear. Every system needs fuel to survive, grow or thrive. Therefore, our culture is a system that needs fuel in the form of energy to continue to go forward and it gets this energy from its people. Since our culture is based on fear, its way of getting this energy is based on control, domination and exploitation. You might say we are like milk cows and our society milks us periodically to get energy (see the article on "Milk Cow Syndrome, p.86).

So, if you like being a milk cow, then, go on and enjoy. However, if you want to be in charge of your life, then you must live differently. I have outlined in this book a way of doing so. I will summarize that way.

1. Adopt the connection/love matrix as your system of choice.

2. Express love with yourself, God (or however you express the supreme-being) and all of God's creations.

3. Just be yourself and let go of the need to create images that you or someone else thinks others might like.

4. Seek to connect with everyone and everything without exploiting, dominating or controlling.

5. Use the Three R's (p. 101) to improve your ability to communicate and understand people.

6. Create what you want in life by (1) knowing what it is that you want (as well as what you don't want); (2) asking God for it (it is said ask and you shall receive); (3) get out the way of it coming to you (you don't have to make it happen, you have to let it happen).

7. Create a homeostatic balance between you and your environment.

8. Help only those who ask for your help; if they have not asked then ask for their permission.

9. Find your place in life, be creative and be the best you can be.

10. Enjoy life, have fun.

Take these items, use them and apply them to your life. At the same time, keep it simple because life was not meant to be a struggle.

Anything is one of a million paths. Therefore, a warrior must always keep in mind that a path is only a path; if he feels that he should not follow it, he must not follow it, he must not stay with it under any conditions. His decision to keep on the path or to leave it must be free of fear or ambition. He must look at every path closely and deliberately. There is a question that a warrior must ask: "Does this path have a heart?"

– The Teachings of Don Juan, Carlos Castaneda

Introduction

This book contains a series of essays and articles that at first glance may seem to be fragmented, unrelated or disjointed. This very idea of fragmentation or disjointedness seems to follow me everywhere I go in one form or another. Most of my life, I have seemed to be out-of-step with those around me. I've often asked, "Where do I fit in?" Or, "Where is my place in life?" Or having college administrators tell me that I can't have a double major in Physics and Music. Or, you can't teach chemistry and psychology courses at the same time. You have to be left-brain or right-brain oriented but not both. Or more recently, "How can you be a "psychic" and a 'management consultant' at the same time?" There are many more. I learned from these experiences to find unique ways of creating what I wanted. This book contains many of those experiences.

I would like to introduce a theme for this book. This theme will be referred to at the beginning of each section and within each essay or article of the book. The theme is "The Synthesis of Thomas III." The word "synthesis" involves an intermingling of components that gives rise to something new and totally different. Synthesis, as it is used here, falls somewhere between making a cake and a salad. In a cake, you take various components, mix thoroughly together, and then bake the mixture to create the cake. When it's done, none of the original components are recognizable. Whereas in making the salad, different components are blended together and once mixed, each component can be recognized and differentiated. The essays in this book are similar to components in a salad. The essays represent diverse experiences and understandings that are very different from each other and yet at the same time "stand alone." Some of these essays have been previously published or used separately in some of my management programs.

At the same time, the chapters in this book represent experiences that have led to my personal growth and development into the person I am today. These experiences represent the components of my life that are similar to baking a cake. As I review my development there are at least five different versions of Thomas. The first version (birth to 25 years of age) can be described as the "Foundation" period of my life; including educational, religious and community experiences. The second version (26 to 37 years of age) represents the "Young Lion" period. This is the period where I was the most creative and lived the "American Dream." The third version (38 to 42 years of age) represents my "Wilderness" Period. This was the transition period of my life, where I remade myself and initiated the process of becoming the person I am today. The fourth version (43 to 60 years of age) represents the "Coming of Age" period. That is the period I started being myself. The fifth version (60+ years of age) represents a state of "Being." My mother always told me, "Just Be Thomas." Thus, we have the "Synthesis of Thomas III."

The components referred to above represent my experiences, understandings and ideas. The development of these components is the result of a unique process that has led me to become the person I am today. This process is unique because it involves a combination of seemingly unrelated fields, such as chemistry, psychology, spirituality and metaphysics. Chemistry and psychology are, of course, "left-brain" oriented; however, even within this sphere of left-braininess, some may find little compatibility between these two. Metaphysics and spirituality are certainly "right-brain" oriented and there may be some conflict between these two as well.

This unique process is also evident in my career experience. My career background includes working as a research engineer, a chemist, a college professor, project manager for a job training program, and director of training in continuing education. This unique process became complete when I developed my prospectus for my doctoral dissertation. I wanted a doctorate that was representative of all my previous experience, an interdisciplinary program.

My preference as a research project was to investigate left-brain/right brain modalities. I was discouraged from using this theme as a project as being beyond the scope of my capabilities at that time. I don't believe the professor really understood what I wanted to do. Two years later he wondered what I was doing with the idea and he wished we had followed up on it. I was so upset I didn't follow up on investigating the reasons for his change of mind.

At any rate, I chose a similar but more philosophical path by developing a new health paradigm that combined the best of the biomedical model (left-brain) and the holistic health model (right-brain) into a new model of health. This model of health as described in the first chapter, "Do I believe in God," has become the theoretical framework for all areas of my life.

Up to this point, I've looked at synthesis in terms of integrating ideas or processes. My ultimate goal in life is to create synthesis within the levels of consciousness of mind, where consciousness can be expressed as a function of three levels, 1) outer, 2) inner and 3) higher.

> The outer conscious level is that part of our mind we are most familiar with because we use it to constantly interact with the outside world. It is the part of the conscious that reinforces reality for most humans. It contains most of the active thought patterns that we learned to use to make day-to-day decisions. These thought patterns are constantly being programmed and/or reinforced by external influences.

> The outer conscious level is said to be analytical, sequential and logic-based.

> The inner conscious level is that part of our mind that contains our knowledge base, past and present. This level of consciousness helps us understand and make sense of our interactions with the world. This level of consciousness is said to be relational, patterned or Gestalt-oriented.

> The higher conscious level is the least known to most humans. It contains the blueprint for our lives and represents our connection to the creator. Thus, this level

of consciousness is where we get our sense of purpose and meaning in life.

I believe that as I am able to successfully integrate or synthesize all three of these levels of consciousness I will have completed my cycle of life on this level of existence. I will therefore be able to evolve to the next level of being.

Even the concept of the Holistic Warrior represents a synthesis. The term, Holistic Warrior can be defined by looking at the individual terms. Holism refers to the idea that a whole is more than the sum of its parts. Further, these parts must also be viewed in terms of how these parts interrelate to each other. A warrior can be defined as one who conquers. In this case, the warrior is not seeking to conquer the outside world but to conquer his or her outer conscious self. That is, seek to integrate the warrior's outer and inner consciousness to create a new conscious whole. This concept is further explained in the first chapter.

I shall use this synthesis to represent not only the integration of ideas and processes but consciousness, as well. This book represents a cathartic approach to not only the past and present events in my life; it also represents my hopes for the future. Therefore, I shall use the idea of synthesis to represent a common theme throughout the development of this book. So, I shall use the theme "The Synthesis of Thomas III," as the glue that ties the essays, stories, ideas, etc. together. There has been only one path for me; however, this path has many lanes that must be seen as interrelated to form a congruent whole.

13

Prologue

The book is based on a set of readings, articles and concept papers I've written over the past twenty-plus years. Some articles or papers were written in response to an event or an experience I encountered or went through. Others were written as a result of an interaction with a friend, a dream, or an idea that came to me. Still other articles have been added to represent understandings that I have developed from life experiences and as a consequence of writing this book. Some have been published in local or regional magazines or newsletters.

Purpose

The purpose of this book of readings is to explain my philosophy of life to my children, grandchildren, and all the rest of the children, grandchildren and great-grandchildren of my parents, Thomas and Evie Nolan. This book is also written for my students, friends, and anyone else who seeks an understanding of life.

It's amazing to me that I have come to be the person I am, different from my siblings because most of them took more traditional paths. I tried the more traditional path in my early years and was quite successful. That period can be called my "Young Lion" years. It was the most creative and active period of my life, and a time when I pursued the American Dream. It didn't seem that way to me at the time, for I never felt comfortable during that period; I just didn't "feel" right. Something was missing, and even today there are many times when I feel that way. Although I did all the right things, all the things I had been taught to do, I didn't do anything for me, personally, the inner "Thomas."

My Evolution

I am the oldest of six living children. I have become an explorer seeking the meaning of life. My goal in life has been to accomplish what I consider to be the ultimate experience — to become like the masters, an enlightened one. Andrew Cohen, the founder of *What is Enlightenment?* Magazine has defined enlightenment this way:

Enlightenment in the time we are living in is not the transcendence of this world, but its transformation, using our very own lives as the vehicles for this most urgent endeavor. It's up to each and every one of us to do whatever we need to do to raise ourselves to a much higher level of engagement with life, so that our very consciousness becomes enlightened with the knowledge of its own meaning and purpose.

In pursuit of this enlightenment much of my early years, my Foundation and Young Lion periods, were spent in frustration and anger because of my perceived circumstances, being born black in a white world. During this period I was extremely arrogant and felt very powerful, yet I was powerless in controlling my destiny. I experienced this powerlessness in my career, relationships and my activist work. In other words, the feeling of power was false because it didn't originate from the inner me. It wasn't until my forties that I began to recognize my personal power, and thus realize that I have choices. Not just any choice, but great choices. I am not always in this state, as some days I feel trapped in a feeling of powerlessness. Fortunately these periods don't last long and I can come into my power again.

But for some time, it seemed that every time I went for the big score — obtaining or keeping jobs or getting the big contract that was to free me — something happened that would cancel or block my progress. I'm not crying because it probably happens to everyone in one way or another. As I look back to that period, it was as though I was being guided or protected to keep me on a previous ordained path. I finally got the message and eventually made deliberate choices to stay on this path at the beginning of my "Wilderness Years."

Wilderness Years

By this time, I knew that my pursuit of the American Dream was not working. And one by one, I had to let go of all the trappings of

15

that dream including religion, marriage, corporate America and my overall allegiance to the "system." It was during this period that I began to search for a better way of dealing with life and I began to write.

My "Wilderness Years" was a period where I experienced a sense of freedom that I hadn't known before and knew only for short periods afterward. I was writing my prospectus for my doctoral program. I had just finished a core course called "Human Ecology" where I was introduced to the holistic health concept. Holistic health was defined in terms of the right brain. Since I could not accept half a brain being a whole, I decided to develop a new holistic health paradigm, and as a result, a philosophy of the universe.

Writing had always been difficult for me, but during this time in my life, I was able to prime the pump. As a result, I developed a connection to a seemingly bottomless well of ideas, a storehouse or virtual database of thoughts and dreams. I found that when properly connected, that is, experiencing my power and choice states, I was able to produce a group of essays. These essays were written in the form of articles and concept papers about events, ideas and my experiences.

Helpful books

Nearly 20 years later, I began compiling these essays into a book. However, I had difficulties putting the book together. I know now that these difficulties occurred because of a missing link in my database, which prevented me from shaping my ideas into a form that made sense to me. This missing link was identified when I was introduced to the book, *Ishmael* by Daniel Quinn. It was a life-changing book because it introduced me to the idea that I, along with most people of the civilized world, have been disconnected from the earth. Civilized people often see themselves as above the laws of nature and view nature as something to subjugate. And, I believe this disconnection is the source of most of the difficulties we experience in creating harmonious relationships, prosperity and peace within our lives.

This book, along with many several other significant books over the past 20 plus years, have helped me create a working model of the universe that helps keep all of my experiences in perspective. I became aware of these books during three stages of the fourth period, the "Coming of Age" period; (1) my awakening; (2) my transforming and (3) my understanding stages.

The books of my awakening stage include *Journey to Ixtlan* by Carlos Castaneda, and *Zen and The Art of Motorcycle Maintenance* and *Lila* by Robert Persig. The books of my transforming stage include *The Celestine Prophecy* and subsequent books by James Redfield; and *The Conversation with God* series and subsequent books by Neal Donald Walsch. Last, and perhaps most important were the books of my understanding stage, *Ishmael* and *The Story of B*, by Daniel Quinn; *Mutant Message Down Under* and *Message From Forever* by Marlo Morgan; and *Like Water for Spirit* by Malidoma Patrice Somé. Of late, another book of equal importance to me has been *The Power of Now* by Eckhart Tolle.

There have been many other books, too numerous to list that have helped me deal with life since my "Wilderness" days in the late 1970s and early 1980s. A list of some of these books will be presented at the end of this book. My "Wilderness Days" was a period of conversion where I left the civilized world and initiated the process of becoming conscious and connected. The following essays and articles have been written as a result of these experiences and my trying to understand how to get the most out of my life. Many books have been written on this topic; some seem to make more sense than others.

It is my hope that the following materials will be useful to you and that you will be able to apply these principles to your everyday life. This book was written with my grandchildren in mind; however, it also represents a working philosophy. I use these materials in my own life, in the readings I conduct with my clients, and in my workshops, seminars, and classes. It has always been my focus to get clients and students to think for themselves; to question what is going on in their lives; to seek ways to get out of their own way; and thus, take responsibility and control of their lives.

Book One

For a warrior, the spirit is an abstract only because he knows it without words or even thoughts. It's an abstract because he can't conceive what the spirit is. Yet, without the slightest chance or desire to understand it, a warrior handles the spirit. He recognizes it, beckons it, entices it, becomes familiar with it, and expresses it with his acts.

— The Power of Silence, Carlos Castaneda

A Philosophy of Life

Everyone has a philosophy. Most people may not be able to articulate what they believe in philosophical terms but it is there nonetheless. Philosophy has always intrigued me; however, most seemed too complicated, obtuse, or impractical for me.

Over the years, I have developed my own philosophy. It has been derived from many sources, 1) my experiences and observations about the world; 2) an eclectic group of books, people and tapes I've read, heard, listened to; 3) the people I've interacted with; and 4) my own understandings from my "Inner Voice." As I have these varied experiences, the information goes into my data bank, where it is processed and comes out uniquely mine.

My best processing mode occurs when I am driving and let go of any need to get where I'm going. This state of mind is achieved primarily on long trips of six hours or longer but occasionally on a shorter trip when it happens spontaneously. It's a state of mind that may be characterized as an altered state. I believe that my outer or conscious mind takes responsibility for driving the car and keeping me safe. Since my conscious mind is driving the car, it is occupied; therefore, my inner or intuitive mind takes over and feeds me information. Some of you may relate to this state of mind as you may get great ideas sometimes while driving to work. These ideas come from a similar source. A more extensive explanation of this "voice" is presented in the essay, The Voice, page 109.

During one of these short trips that occurred during the end of my Wilderness Years Period (see the section Two Paths to Spirituality, page 163). I realized I needed a philosophy. Immediately, it occurred to me that the underpinnings of a workable philosophy had been created with the writing of my dissertation prospectus. An explanation of this philosophy is presented in the next essay. It was like a voice within saying, Duh! What have you been working on these past few years? So, began the foundations of The Philosophy according to Thomas III.

22

The foundation of this philosophy is presented in the form of three essays; 1) "Do I Believe in God?" 2) Adam and Eve; and 3) "The Chicken and the Eagle". The first essay in the "The Synthesis of Thomas III" came about because I ask the question "Do I believe in God?" I asked this question of myself one evening as I was driving on I-35 south toward my home in Norman, OK. It was a short trip and that spontaneous state of mind appeared. Sometimes this spontaneous state of mind appears from just looking at the sky, a group of trees, or a field as I drive down the highway. I make a connection with the particular area of focus and I am automatically "there!"

I had just completed a workshop at Langston University in Langston, OK, sixty miles north of Norman. It was nighttime and the sky was clear. It must have been around January-February because the constellation Orion's Belt was high in the southern sky at 9:00 p.m. Orion's Belt has a unique meaning for me because of an experience I had in Santa Fe, several years before, my call to the ministry (See the essay, "Three Modes of Thomas" page 130).

As I looked at Orion's Belt, I began to think about the enormity of the universe and led to thoughts about God. Many times before I had thought about how the universe, life, and everything was put together. I realized then that although I had professed a belief in God, I had never challenged that belief. I didn't know if the belief was because I was raised to believe or if the belief was true within my heart. I was just beginning to understand the heart/gut relationship as a means for dealing life's trials and tribulations (see the essay, "Feelings" page 94). That is, no matter what I am experiencing at the time. If I have a heart feeling, I know I'm going to be okay. If I have a gut feeling then something is wrong; the intensity of that feeling lets me know how quickly I need to act upon the feeling. So, I posed the question and several weeks later an answer came. I knew within my heart, I truly did believe in God. As a result, I wrote the essay "Do I believe in God?"

Many of the ideas that later became an essay or tool in my work came about as a result of some interaction with a friend or in small group discussions. One such interaction was with a friend named Roy, in Santa Fe during the early nineties. It had to do with a discussion of the Adam and Eve story. I met Roy during an art fair held over a Labor Day weekend. I was sitting on a park bench on the "Square" in downtown Santa Fe, across from his display. He carved birds and other figures out of wood. We began talking and became friends. Roy had a unique way of carving his figures and as we discussed how he carved them I realized that he was able to achieve a similar state of mind as I did while driving during his carving. We talked about many things but somehow we began to discuss the Adam and Eve story.

We met several times after then and during one of those discussions, I gained some insight about the inner meaning of the creation of Adam and Eve and what it means in terms of the integration and evolution of consciousness among humans. Three separate ideas or concepts came together; (1) The Adam and Eve story, second chapter of Genesis; (2) The last verse of the Book of Thomas from the Nag Hammadi scrolls; and (3) Interaction within the nucleus of an atom.

I had recently read the "Book of Thomas". And, since I also have a background in Chemistry, I believe I had a unique perspective that integrated the above three concepts together. As Roy and I discussed the Adam and Eve Story, three separate and seemingly different ideas surfaced and came together, 1) the last verse from the Book of Thomas; 2) how the nucleus of the atom stays together; and 3) the Adam and Eve Story. Thus, I gained a new understanding of the Adam and Eve Story. This discussion represents the first process that led to the "Synthesis of Thomas III." It helped me to gain a better idea of why I am here and what I want to accomplish in this life. This synthesis applies not only to me but also to anyone looking for enlightenment or to achieve a higher level of consciousness.

Sometimes there are strong conflicts between the Outer conscious or "programmed" self and the Inner or "inner-led" conscious self. The programmed self represents the way we have been trained by the civilized world to act. The Inner conscious self represents the way an individual acts because he or she has decided to make a conscious, deliberate, choice in all situations.

The Chicken and The Eagle, page 44, story represents the transformation from the programmed self to the "inner-led" conscious self. It also represents two different directions one can take during the subjugation process. One person may accept his or her lot and identify with the subjugator, while the other person resists. This is not to indict one or make a martyr out of the other. Dealing with life is about the choices we make and the choices we make are dependent on whether the waters of life are below the knees or above the waist. When the waters are above the knees, survival is the only thing that matters and there are very few choices and none of them good. When the waters are below the knees, we have few choices and most are in our favor. There by the grace of God, I have been blessed with many choices.

The combination of the two essays and the Chicken and Eagle story represents a desire to have a firm foundation, a stated purpose or goal, and the desire to be free to pursue that goal. Thus, we have the development of a philosophical foundation for the "Synthesis of Thomas III."

Do I Believe in God?

The answer is an unqualified "Yes!" However, you might ask, "Why do I believe in God?" (In order to get the right answer, you must ask the right question.) How can we make sense of the second question? We need to make sense of this question because it forms the foundation for living a full, productive, and enriched life. The answer to the second question might be best answered in terms of determining a "Proof of the existence of God."

Proof of the Existence of God

When I want proof of the existence of God, I need only look around me at God's creations. Three examples within the creative processes come to mind, 1) Gravitation forces; 2) the autopoiesis process; and 3) the specific rules that causes particles to make choices to form more complex particles. An example of the gravitation can be observed by looking at an eclipse of the moon. Next time you have an opportunity, take a look. When I look at the moon, under normal conditions, it is hard to distinguish it from the sky. It's like being a part of the landscape picture. However, when I observed the moon during an eclipse some time during the early eighties; the Moon seemed to be just hanging there and there was nothing holding it up. If the Moon is just hanging there, then so is the earth, the Sun, and all those other objects in space. Now, I know the scientific explanation that has to do with force of gravity. But that leads to a whole litany of questions; so, what holds the Sun up, the Milky Way Galaxy; then what holds the Milky Way Galaxy up and so on? We can break it down to a simple question, "what is the source of this gravitation pull?" "Who or what initiated this force?" In other words, something is responsible for this force.

The second example is the autopoietic process. It can be found in all natural systems and all living things. Autopoiesis refers to the characteristic that living systems have to continuously renew themselves and to regulate this process in such a way that the integrity of their structure is maintained. We have created autopoietic mechanical and social entities. That is, we have been able to model the autopoietic process but not reproduce this process. We can facilitate autopoiesis but we can't create it. Something is responsible for this autopoietic process.

The third example involves inanimate objects. So, let us look at atoms and molecules, the smallest forms of matter that can stand-alone. What causes these particles to make the choices they do to combine in specific ways according to specific rules of engagement to form more complex particles? These rules of engagement are based on some type of consciousness, such that, as these particles combine to form more and more complex aggregates, the consciousness of these particles also become more and more complex until at some point that particle becomes alive, as we know it. Who is responsible for this consciousness?

There are many examples we could choose on all levels of existence. There are worlds within worlds, macro and micro processes that are comparable to the processes with living matter. All these worlds show some type of orderedness, and/or rules of engagement that are somehow similar. Somehow, all of these worlds are also connected. So, who or what is responsible for these events or processes?

So, when I want proof of God's existence, I just look around me. The natural world is full of examples that I can take as proof of a higher organizing power. I choose to call this higher power, God.

Operational Definitions of God

I consider myself now to be spiritual rather than religious. I was brought up in a religious environment and as a result have a solid foundation of faith in God from this experience. I was a child then. As I became more mature, I recognized that this set of beliefs, faith, as it were, was not enough. You see, religion to me is like being in the third grade and I want to be a post-graduate student of life. I use this reference to show that I am looking within for guidance rather than some reference outside of me.

To me, there is a big difference between being religious and being spiritual. Let me therefore define this difference. This definition is based on a set of understandings produced from my life experiences. Throughout my life I have made my own definitions about the way things are and have used these definitions to help me navigate through life. These definitions, by necessity may or may not agree with textbook or recognized definitions.

Religion can be defined as looking outside of one's self for guidance. That is, God is out there and I am here. In other words, God and I are separate. Therefore, I must bring God inside of me. Since God is outside of me, religion is there to intercede for me for I am not worthy or capable of making that decision for myself. I am therefore seen as a sheep and must have the shepherd to care of me.

Spirituality can be defined as looking within me for guidance. I believe that God is the sum total of everything in the universe and more. Therefore, if God is everything and more, then, God is also a part of everything and everything is a part of God. Simply, God and I are one. Now, that idea is good news to me because it lets me know that I am a part of God and God is also a part of me. Therefore, I can find God within me!

I have a connection to the most powerful force in the universe. I am not alone. I have a source of power that I can tap into at will or at least when I can remember to do so. I have been given free will to explore the dimensions of the universe to gain experiences and discover who I am. God is indeed, outside of me however and more importantly, I don't have to go outside of myself to find God. I need only to look inside of me.

So, let us look at a more comprehensive definition of God. I realize that some religious or spiritual traditions like the Tao, believe that God can't be defined. So, instead of a textbook or constitutive definition, I would like to present operational or working definitions. In fact, I would like to present three working definitions because they have provided me with the firm foundation I've needed to live, grow, and thrive as a sentient being. (The wise person builds his house on the Rock). The working definitions are as follows:

1. My prospectus for research on my doctorate work, written more than 20 years ago

2. My observations about nature and thus, the world

3. Walsh's explanation of God from his book, "Conversations with God.

Research Prospectus for Doctoral Program

God can be defined in terms of the universe, since the universe can be seen as "all that is", and God has been defined as "All That Is." A definition of God emerged while I was working on a basic notion of health during the development of my doctoral prospectus. I sought to develop a foundation for showing the universe in terms of a system or better still to show the universe as systems within systems; and human beings as one of those systems within systems. If the universe was to be described in this way, then I had to have a way of defining the universe in terms of a set of systems; and, more importantly in terms of relationships between these sets of systems. So, I used a set three basic concepts that would best describe the relationships between different components or subsets of systems within the universe. I will explain these concepts later in this discussion. Of course, one of these subsets would describe how humans interacted within their environment as a part of the universe.

The use of three basic concepts to describe the universe can be best justified by referring to the Tao Te Ching by Lao-Tzu, specifically Verse 42. The first few lines of verse 42 read as follows:

Tao gives birth to One;

One gives birth to Two;

Two gives birth to Three.

Three gives birth to the Ten Thousand Things.

These four lines form the basic format of a model of the universe I developed 33 years ago, even before I knew the Tao Te Ching existed. When we look at the description of the creation of man, as well as, of Adam and Eve in the Christian Bible, we can see

29

the same format. The creation of man follows the first two lines (Man, represents both male and female) while the creation of Adam and Eve follows the first three lines, as we will explain in the next chapter. In other words, we have the concept of a trinity, between Adam, Eve, and "the creative force."

The trinity is an important way of defining God in Christianity, as well as, many other religious institutions. We can also see this same format in science when we look at the smallest particle that can stand alone, the atom. Within the nucleus of the atom, there are neutrons and protons. There is a third particle outside the nucleus, the electron. The interactions between these three components give rise to all things in the physical world. And, I might add, I am a third generation of Thomas James Nolan in my family.

It seems to me then, that this one, two, three or three format is an excellent way of delineating the idea of God. So, I will use this format to define a model God and the universe. I will use the model I developed while writing the prospectus for my dissertation more than twenty-five years ago. This Model of God can be described as follows:

A Model of God
1. <u>Wholistic</u> – Expressed as a singular unified omnipotent being (i.e., the "creator."
2. <u>Dualistic</u> – This being can be described in two basic forms: One based on separateness and one connectedness (i.e., matter and energy).
3. <u>Trinistic</u> – Each basic form can be expressed as three levels of being: the levels above, the levels below, and the level of operation. (i.e., humans: levels below – humans have similar internal environments; levels above – share a common external environment; and the level of operation – the human itself).

The word, trinistic, was created from the word trinity to parallel the terms wholistic and dualistic, correspond to with the end-forms of the words whole (Wholistic) and dual (Dualistic). By combining these three components, we now have the basic ingredients that lead us to a development of a model of the universe that I will call "The Holistic Model of the Universe."

Figure 1
The Holistic Model Of The Universe

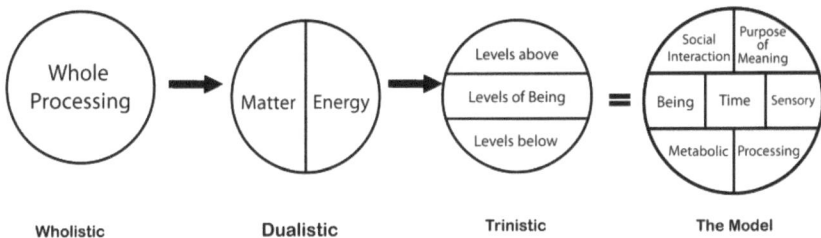

| Wholistic | Dualistic | Trinistic | The Model |

The Holistic Model of the Universe

a) Wholistic – The universe is seen as an integrated and hierarchical whole. Integration refers to interrelationship, while hierarchical refers to increased complexity and order as the universe evolves to higher levels.

(Examples: a person, a building, or the ocean)

b) Dualistic – The universe is seen in terms of the Matter and Energy dichotomy; thus, matter and energy are two forms of the same thing they cannot be created or destroyed but converted one to another. Matter can be further expressed as parts, creating the worldview of separateness; while energy can be expressed in terms of interrelationships, creating the worldview of connectedness.

Examples:

Matter	Energy
A family	The interactions between the family members;
A flock of birds	The patterns formed while flying; or oceans/the wave energy created by the motion of within the ocean)

c) Trinistic – The hierarchical universe is seen as the level above, the levels below, and levels of operation; both Matter and Energy are each expressed as three levels of being; matter, as the level of operation, is seen in terms of wholes that are composed of integrated and hierarchical subsystems where each system can be seen at the same time as a subset of higher systems (levels above) and yet composed of systems themselves (levels below); energy can be seen in terms of the interactions, relationships, or connectedness of these systems. These levels of being as systems also imply the concept of time. Therefore, we can add the trinistic concept of past, present, and future.

(Example: person

Matter	Energy
The family unit, community, etc.	The values, beliefs, and represents the levels of above; mores
The person represents	The gathering of data the level of being; using the senses
The subsystems within the, person	Mental and emotional circulatory, respiratory

32

represents the processing modes, i.e., the levels below

Thus, God is defined in terms of a unified whole, (One). The unified whole can then be seen in terms of two basic webs or networks (Two), one based on separateness and one based on connectedness. Both the separateness and connectedness networks can then be seen as having three levels of expressions along a hierarchy (Three); the level of operation that expresses itself as the level of beingness; the levels above that forms more complex forms of beingness; and the levels below that forms less complex forms of beingness.

My Observations about Nature and Thus, the World

During the month of December 2000, I was driving to Dallas from Norman on I-35 passing through the Arbuckle Mountains. As I drove through these mountains, I remembered to quiet my mind and as a result I became aware of my Inner Voice, an article about this 'Voice", (page 109) will be presented later in the section, "Operating in Life." The Voice directed me to focus on the growing vegetation on either side of the road. I was able to focus not only on the vegetation on either side of the road, but the many forms of life there. I became aware that this vegetation and other forms of life grow whether we want it to or not. And that all around me, life was abundant and flourishing. Thus, I become aware of what Daniel Quinn speaks of as the "Community of Life" or what most humans call, nature.

I became aware of the relationship between humans and our environment. Humans have built roads, buildings, etc. in this community of life for thousands of years. However, as soon as, humans leave these roads, buildings, etc., this "community of life" reclaims these areas. The question posed to me by the Voice, "Who or what controls this process?"

There are parallel processes within our bodies. We have little or no conscious control of our bodies, that is, we can't control (i.e., consciously stop and restart) the systems within our bodies. All of these functions are maintained by some internal process that is similar in all forms of life on this planet. I further became aware that this process is not unique to our planet but present through the universe in one form or another. We can influence these processes but we can't create them. Again the Voice posed the question, "Who or what controls these processes?"

We can describe these functions as natural or living systems. Natural systems can be described in terms of a set of coherent, evolving, interactive processes that temporarily manifest in globally stable structures that have nothing to do with the equilibrium and the solidity of technological structures. These natural systems can be further described in terms of dissipative structures, the concept of autopoiesis, and the process of randomness.

Dissipative structures refers to chemical reaction type systems which themselves maintain energy and matter penetration of globally stable structures over extended periods of time. They are flow dependent structures that streamline energy flow making it more efficient. Living systems are dissipative in that they are highly organized and open whole entities in continuous flow toward and in constant need of energy. These systems maintain continuous entropy (movement toward disorder) production and dissipate the accruing entropy. These systems are further referred to as in a state of nonequilibrium (moving away from equilibrium to maintain stability and growth).

Autopoiesis refers to the characteristic of living systems to continuously renew them and to regulate this process in such a way that the integrity of their structure is maintained.

Randomness refers to the degrees of freedom available to the system for the self-determination of its own evolution and for finding its temporary optimal stability under given starting conditions.

The central aspects of these three factors describe a self-organizing universe in terms of (1) specific macroscopic dynamics of process systems (interactions in the world we see),

(2) continuous exchanges and thereby co-evolution within the environment, and (3) self-transcendence, the evolution of evolutionary processes. Again, "Who or what controls these processes?"

Neal D. Walsch's explanation of God from his book "Conversations with God:

Many times we find definitions as presented by others not only correspond to our own definitions but also may do a better job. Such is the case by Neal Donald Walsch in his book, "Conservations with God." Walsch's book is unique in that it was dictated by an internal presence that expresses itself through automatic writing is similar to the Inner Voice, only instead of a voice inside of your head; your inner conscious state uses your hand to write messages. He defines God as follows:

> In the beginning there was an energy known as "All That Is". This energy knew "all that was" and at the same time "all that was not." However, this energy, "All That Is", did not know experience. In order to know experience, "All That Is" operated on itself and split into two parts; that which was based on connectedness and love; and that which was based on separation and fear. Love interacts with itself and as fear interacts with itself, and as love and fear interacts with each other, experience is created.

As we look at all three definitions, we get a much more complete understanding of the nature of God, and the universe. All three definitions come from different perspectives, yet they all begin with some unit force that everything else emanates from without contradiction. Out of these three definitions, we also see that we have a choice as to which perspectives we want to live by. It's so happens that each perspective can be explained by some system living or otherwise on this planet. Indigenous cultures, i.e., Native Americans, Australian Aborigines, the native peoples of sub-Sahara Africa, etc., before colonization, live by the rule of connectivity, that is, they see themselves as connected, as natural and integral parts of their environment.

I am not trying to glorify indigenous cultures; they have many of the same problems that civilized people do. The difference is the concept of connectivity. Civilized cultures like the one we live in, live by the rule of separation and fear. We protect ourselves by exploiting, controlling, and/or dominating our environment because we believe that otherwise we will be exploited, controlled, and/or dominated by our environment.

Actually, I perceive a third choice of cultures. I certainly don't like the idea of separation and fear or the idea of exploitation, control, or domination. At the same time, although I really admire the indigenous cultures, I really like the comfort, as well as, many of the technological advances of the civilized world. Therefore, I postulate a third choice that integrates the best of both worlds that seeks the connectivity of the indigenous cultures and the technological advances of the civilized that are non-threatening to the environment. I call this third choice, "The Balanced Matrix." I will explain more about this balanced matrix in the latter chapters of this book.

This third choice, "The Balance Matrix," offers a cultural base that contains my "inner group" of friends. This "inner group" is composed of people who think like me and accept me unconditionally. This group can also be defined as tribal as defined by Caroline Myss. Ms. Myss, in her book, Anatomy of the Spirit, discussed chakra points in the body. Chakra points are energy centers in the body that represents points of balance and transformation. She relates these chakra points to life events, processes, and experiences. She discusses the first chakra, the "Root Chakra" as the chakra of the tribe. That is, it represents the group of people that has the most influences how a person acts. For instance, sometimes a person wants to achieve a goal that is not approved by the group. When that happens, the group may sabotage or prevent that person from accomplishing that goal. Thus, the person must give up the goal or find a new group that supports his or her goals. In "The Synthesis of Thomas III," The Balanced Matrix offers a group of people that supports my growth and development.

An Adam and Eve Allegory:
The Second Creation Story

Every Christian all over the world knows the story of Adam and Eve. Most take this story literally. There are beliefs about the relationship between the sexes, derived from this story that support dominance of males, which in turns stirs a lot of emotions. I believe however that there are hidden mysteries around this story that most people and perhaps the clergy don't understand. This article represents my interpretation of the hidden mystery behind the story of Adam and Eve.

My interpretation centers on three totally and apparently different constructs; (1) The nucleus of the atom; (2) The first line and last verse of the Book of Thomas from the Nag Hammadi scrolls; and (3) the concepts of Man and Male. This interpretation became apparent during a discussion with a friend in Santa Fe, NM.

Let us explore some assumptions about the words, Adam, man, and male, as well as, some definitions about the atom. We will then relate Adam, man, and male to an explanation of the inner working of an atom. Many of the problems that deal with Man and Adam are based on how each is defined or used in representations. The current use of each term causes a lot of confusion and makes interpretations very difficult. Later, we will also explore the concept of male.

First, the atom can be defined as a unified whole. In science, atom is referred to as the smallest particle that can stand alone. Man as presented in Genesis, Chapter I, also is a unified whole. In verse 27, Man was created as both male and female; therefore, Man is not male but androgynous. In other words, man can be seen like the atom as a unified whole, as well.

Next, let us look at some assumptions about Adam and Eve. Before we review these assumptions, I would like to make an allegory using the inter-relationships between the neutrons, protons, electrons, and beta particles of an atom. Neutrons and protons are found in the nucleus and electrons exist in probable states in space around this nucleus. Most people don't know that electrons are also found in the nucleus. They are referred to as Beta (ß) particles. Neutrons have a neutral or zero charge, while protons have positive and electrons and beta particles have negative charges, respectively.

In order to create stability in the nucleus, neutrons are constantly breaking down into protons and beta particles and at the same time protons and beta particles are recombining to form neutrons such that an equilibrium exist between them. The reactions are written as shown as follows:

Neutron $\rightleftarrows$ proton (p^+) + beta particle (β^-)

or

$n^0 \longrightarrow p^+ + \beta^-$

$p^+ + \beta^- \longrightarrow n^0$

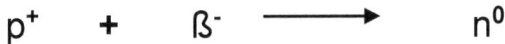

The mass of the neutron is defined as 1. The mass of the proton is defined as approximately 1 (~1), because the mass of the Beta particle is defined as 1/1280 that of the mass of the neutron.

It should be noted that when the neutron breaks up into the proton and beta particle, the proton has essentially the same mass and has been assigned a mass of one (1). The proton also has a positive (+) charge. In other words, the proton is seen as a different entity from the neutron. We will come back to these examples later.

The allegory can be explained as follows:

Let Adam be defined in terms of the neutron as described in the previous paragraphs. Then, when Adam was created, Adam was whole, having both positive and negative energies.

Since Adam did not have a mate, Lord God took one of his ribs and created Eve. Current interpretations show that only two beings were thus involved, Adam and his new mate, Eve. Now, if we use the neutron particle analogy, instead of having two beings or particles created, we actually have three.

> For instance, when the neutron splits to form a proton and an electron, it is not called the neutron and electron because the neutron is not the same as it was before. It is now two new particles, a proton and an electron.

> So, when Eve was created from Adam, two new beings were created instead of one. A new Adam (Adam II) and Eve. Or,

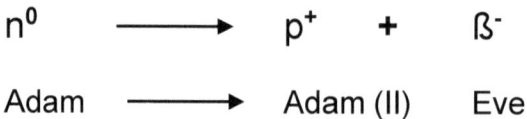

$$n^0 \longrightarrow p^+ + \beta^-$$

Adam $\longrightarrow$ Adam (II)   Eve

Now, with this new interpretation, we can see that the term Adam needs to be redefined. Adam should be defined in this specific case as a whole being having both male and female attributes and energies.

With this new interpretation, we can better understand most passages in the Bible and other sacred books. Genesis, Chapter One, the creation of spiritual Man (or spiritual being) refers to man as a whole being with both masculine and femmine energies. Genesis, Chapter Two, the creation of physical man, Adam, was created as a whole being, have both masculine and femmine energies.

When Eve was created, she was created from Adam's rib. Adam, then, is no longer the same being. Adam has become two different beings, a new Adam (Adam II) and Eve. As in the neutron analogy, the neutron is no longer the same because it has become two new particles a proton and a beta particle. The neutron is not called a neutron, once this split has taken place, because it is now two different particles.

Further, if we make a comparison between the beta particle and Adam's rib, we see another analogy between the two. An assumption is made that since only the rib was taken it was so small compared to the whole that Adam remains the same.

So, if we compare equations, we have as follows:

The Current Understanding	**The New Understanding**
	$n^0 \longrightarrow p^+ \quad + \quad \beta^-$
Adam $\longrightarrow$ Adam + Eve	Adam (0) $\longrightarrow$ Adam(II) + Eve

The ultimate significance of this new understanding is shown in Genesis, Chapter 2, verse 24, where it reads as follows:

Verse 24) - Therefore shall a man leave his father and mother and shall cleave unto his wife, and they shall be one flesh.

Now, let us go back to the original equilibrium relationship between the neutron, proton, and beta particle.

Neutron $\rightleftharpoons$ proton (p^+) $+$ beta particle (β^-)

or

$$n^0 \longrightarrow p^+ \quad + \quad \beta^-$$

$$p^+ \quad + \quad \beta^- \longrightarrow n^0$$

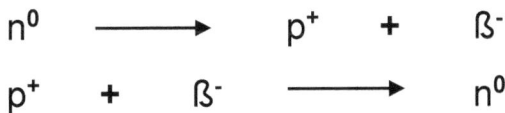

The reason the nucleus is able to maintain stability, is that two opposite reactions take place at the same time: (1) the neutron splits into a proton and a beta particle and (2) a separate proton and beta particle recombines to form a new neutron.

We have described Adam becoming Adam (II) and Eve, in terms of the neutron breaking up into the proton and beta particle. But what about the reverse, when the proton and beta particle recombines to form a new neutron?

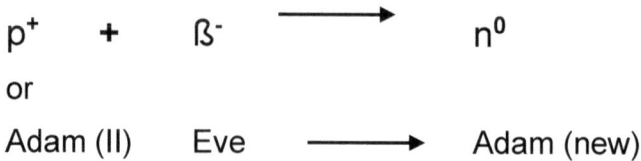

$$p^+ \quad + \quad \beta^- \quad \longrightarrow \quad n^0$$

or

Adam (II)   Eve $\longrightarrow$ Adam (new)

The explanation can be seen in two forms:

<u>The Physical Plane</u>
When Adam (II) and Eve come together on the physical plane, a new life or baby is created.

<u>The Spiritual Plane</u>
When Adam (II) and Eve come together on the spiritual plane, a new and higher consciousness is created.

In other words, Adam (II) leaves his mother and father, both embodied within Adam; and rejoins with Eve to create a new Adam on a higher plane of consciousness, just as Jesus did when he became the Christ.

We can now look at the concept of male and how it has been misinterpreted at times, as well. There is a document found in the Nag Hammadi scrolls, called "The Gospel According to Thomas". The first line of this book reads as follows:

Jesus said: He who uncovers the significance of these words shall not taste death.

It would seem to me that this statement implies that what follows is very important to one's spiritual development. Next, let us visit the last verse of this book, verse 114 (in particular the second sentence). It reads as follows:

Simon Peter said to them, "Let Mary leave us, for women are not worthy of Life."

Jesus said, "I myself shall lead her in order to make her <u>male</u>, so that she too may become a living spirit *resembling you <u>males</u>. For every woman who will make herself <u>male</u> will enter the kingdom of heaven."*

This last paragraph should read when interpreted properly, as follows:

Jesus said, "I myself shall lead her in order to transform her into a **whole person**, so that she too may become a living spirit resembling you **who have been transformed**. For every woman and **every person** who will make **themselves**, **whole**, will enter the Kingdom of Heaven."

Male in this case does not refer to gender but refers to a transformation to wholeness. The Disciples had already undergone a transformation to wholeness or a higher consciousness before. Whether Man or male in these specific cases, were mistakenly translated or made cryptic on purpose is unknown. I will refer the reader to the first line of the Gospel According to Thomas. Therefore, Man, male, and Adam in this case refer to a concept of wholes.

Thus, as I travel my own path, my goal is to become a **Whole Person**. This rest of this book is dedicated in one way or another to expressing or demonstrating my path toward this transformation to wholeness. This path, then, becomes an outcome statement in describing the essence of "The Synthesis of Thomas III".

The Chicken And The Eagle
The Story

The Chickens decided one day, as they watched the soaring Eagle, that they would do an experiment. The purpose of this experiment would be to make an Eagle think it is a Chicken, and therefore, show this magnificent bird who the real rulers are.

The Chickens, then, captured some Eagles and were moderately successful in making the Eagles act like Chickens; however, when the Eagles got tired of the game, they would fly away.

The Chickens not to be out done then stole two Eagle eggs and after the incubation period raised the hatched Eaglets as though they were Chickens. This time, the Chickens were very successful, for the Eaglets actually believe they were Chickens although the Eaglets were puzzled and knew something was very wrong. They were golden brown, lean, and strong but the Chickens were cream colored, fat, and weak. The Eaglets didn't know any better, so they thought something was wrong with them. But that's just the way it was supposed to be.

The two eaglets were named Tom and Thomas. Tom liked the situation and even though he felt the intense hatred, heard the snide remarks, and felt uncomfortable he felt he was taken care of. He had food to eat, a place to sleep, and although the Chickens mistreated him, it wasn't so bad a situation. Thomas on the other hand, was rebellious, he knew he didn't fit in and sometimes in fits of rage he would go running through the yard and take off flying. These short flights would scare him to death. None of the other Chickens could do that, so something must be wrong with him to be able to do such a thing. He couldn't get along with the other "chicks", so he became a loner. He tried to talk to Tom, but Tom was too content with the situation to hear what Thomas had to say.

One day while Thomas was in the yard, he saw a speck high in the sky above the Chicken yard. The speck grew larger and larger, until it became a very large bird that looked suspiciously like Thomas. The bird flew in and perched on a tree limb above Thomas. The bird spoke to Thomas and said, "Boy? What are you doing down there? Don't you know who you are?" Thomas replied back, "I'm a Chicken and I live here." The very large bird laughed and said, "A Chicken! Now I've heard it all, you've got to be joking! How in the world can you think you are a Chicken?" Thomas said, "Well, that is what I've been told by the others, my parents, and other chickens as well." The Eagle laughed again, now he was a wise old bird and didn't want to scare Thomas too badly. So, the Eagle said, "Well, what do you think I am?" Thomas said, "I don't know, you look a little like me, only much larger and you can fly. I don't know who you are, you are strange!" The Eagle said to Thomas, "I am an Eagle, I come from a royal family of birds who are meant to fly majestically over all other beings, we are Kings and Queens. Look at yourself; you've already admitted you look like me, YOU ARE AN EAGLE!" Thomas said in awe, "I AM!" "I knew something was different about me but I couldn't tell what it was. I AM AN EAGLE! WOW!"

The Eagle told Thomas to fly up to the tree limb and join him. Thomas replied, "I can't fly". The Eagle said to Thomas, "You have royal blood in your veins, you are a King, spread your wings and fly!" Thomas tried and tried; each time he got closer and closer to the branch, until he finally made it. He was exhausted. As he was catching his breath, the wise old Eagle began to tell him about his heritage, who he really was and about his destiny.

A little later, Tom came under the limb and saw Thomas on the tree branch, He exclaimed! "Thomas! What are you doing up there, and who's that strange bird with you, a buzzard or something? Get down before you hurt yourself." Thomas said to Tom, "Tom you know what, we are Eagles. We've been duped. We have the blood of Kings and Queens in our veins." Tom said, "Un huh! Sure, get down from there before you get us in trouble!" Thomas said to Tom, "Come up here with us." Tom said, "I'm not coming up there, I might hurt myself. You're as crazy as that large buzzard there with you."

The wise old Eagle knew it was time to go, he said, "It's time to go, Thomas. We must leave." Thomas pleaded with Tom "come with us, there's a whole new world out there, beautiful, rich, and magnificent." Tom said, "What? Leave here, why? I don't for a minute believe that old buzzard. I've got good food, a place to sleep, and Chickens to talk to, besides, my world is right here!" Thomas again pleaded with Tom to come, but the wise old Eagle said to Thomas, "Sometimes, we have to leave loved ones behind, they have their own life and destiny. Until they can see things for themselves and be willing to take risks to find out who they are, we must leave them behind."

The wise old Eagle and Thomas flew off. As they flew for a while, Thomas began to get tired. The Eagle said, "Son, you have the strength of Kings and Queens in your blood, reach down deep within yourself and **fly!**" Soon, as they were crossing a very large river, raging along its pathway, Thomas became afraid the Eagle said, "Look, that's the river of fear and the unknown, you must conquer your fears and frustrations, remember you have the blood of Kings and Queens, **spread your wings and fly!**" After, a while they came upon a large mountain. Thomas almost was overcome by the high altitude. The Wise old bird said, "This is the mountain of prejudice; overcoming the illusions of others, remember you have royal blood in your veins; you determine your own reality, pull yourself together, gather your wits and **fly!**" After they flew over the mountain, and were at last headed home there were deep drops with treacherous winds and currents. Thomas was almost sucked in. The wise old Eagle said, "This is the greatest obstacle, it's the winds and currents of self-doubt and anxiety, reach down deep within yourself, find that inner strength, relax, remember you have the heritage of the greatest and most regal beings of them all, **SPREAD YOUR WINGS AND FLY!**

THOMAS SAID, "I AM AN EAGLE" AND FLEW OFF TO MEET HIS DESTINY!

The illusions of the outside world (The Chickens) are always providing each one of us with a comfort zone. This comfort is actually a trap, a jail cell as it were, that keeps us from exploring who we really are. In the first essay of this book, I discussed Caroline Myss' ideas about the "Root Chakra," the chakra of the tribe. The tribes we belong to determine our reality. When we are dependent (most of us don't even know we are), we need the tribe. It creates illusions that provide a false sense of security (any security that comes from external sources is false). This false sense of security turns us into sheep that is dependent on the shepherd for their well-being or at best a pawn, expendable to the outside world.

This story demonstrates a need to wake up. However, I find that most people are like Tom and are not ready to wake-up and contrary to the beliefs of the religionists, it is not my or your job to wake them up. It is written that when the pupil is ready, the teacher (the wise old eagle) will appear. More importantly, in the world based on "The Eagle" and "The Synthesis of Thomas III," there is no need to save anyone because they already are! We all are whole! We are already there!

The belief that we are separate is the basis for the great illusion of the outside world of "The Chicken." When you believe that you are separate there is no way to play a "Win-Win" lifestyle because you have to depend on others for your well-being. Therefore, you must play "Win-Lose" lifestyle. Most people don't really understand the nature of the Win-Lose game. That is, the absolute only way for anyone to win is for someone else to lose. Thus, you must be able to do anything it takes to win. Many, perhaps, most of us are not willing to do that and if you are not, you are going to lose unless you change lifestyles. Unfortunately, we have been programmed by the outside world (The Chickens) to play the Win-Lose lifestyle. However, there is another way. I shall discuss more about that lifestyle in a later essay, "Two Worlds: Connectedness and Separateness.

In "The Synthesis of Thomas III," I have made a conscious choice to be "The Eagle" and I constantly work on discovering and removing old patterns from my chicken era. A summary of both philosophies of The Chicken and the Eagle are shown in Table I.

TABLE I

PHILOSOPHY ACCORDING TO
THE CHICKEN AND THE EAGLE[1]

Philosophy of the Chicken	Philosophy of the Eagle
We lack something	We lack nothing; we have everything and are everything
We need something outside ourselves to make us feel secure, happy and worth something as a person	The source of security and happiness comes from within
When you give something, you lose it	As you give, you must also receive and as a result you become blessed many times over
Seek and do not find	Seek and you shall find
We are a body	We are Body, Mind, and Spirit
We are a sinner	We are all, Children of GOD
We are separate beings	We are ONE with everything and "All That Is"
We are destroyed by death	Life is eternal
The motivation and glue that holds us together are fear, separation, judgment, anger, and guilt.	The motivation and glue that holds us together are love, connection, freedom, peace, and joy.

[1] Adapted from the Book, From a Chicken to an Eagle by Jerry Frankhauser (1983)

Human beings are perceivers, but the world they perceive is an illusion: an illusion created by the description that was told to them from the moment they were born.

So, in essence, the world that their reason wants to sustain is the world created by a description and its dogmatic and inviolable rules, which their reason learns to, accept and defend.

– Tales of Power, Carlos Castaneda

Perception/Perspectives

One of the most effective communication tools I have used in conducting management workshops is the 3R's (an essay in the section on "Operating in Life). The first "R" is based on the question, "What is? Or What is the Nature of Reality?" Reality in this case refers to how we utilize our perceptions and perspective. Sometimes, as we have seen in the previous section, these perceptions and perspectives are based on programmed responses. So, it is in our best interest to challenge how we view the world. Thus, the next step in the development of the "Synthesis of Thomas III" is to show (1) how we might get trapped in a given perspective; (2) to question reality as we perceive it to determine if it indeed serves us; and (3) how we can apply this information to our lifestyles.

Although the following essays were written and published more than 20 years ago, I believe they will offer a perspective that will be useful today. The Emperor's New Clothes, Revisited addresses the issue of the need to question reality. One of the questions that we need to constantly ask is "Does our current reality serve us?" In other words, does it help us meet our needs, goals, and desires? Because if it doesn't then the basis of our reality, that is, how we view the world, needs to be changed until it does serve us. Do we realize that much of what we believe or how we express ourselves is programmed? Or are beliefs based on old patterns of behavior that are no longer part of our current perceptions or perspective. I also remember a phrase I heard years ago, "Hypnotized by our own beliefs!"

The second essay was written in response to a self-imposed question. This question is based on a belief that I choose my birth, birthplace, parents, as well as, specific events or conditions that I will encounter during my lifetime. So, it occurred to me that maybe something was wrong with this choice; why would I choose such harsh and near impossible conditions? Much of my earlier life was filled with anger because of these conditions; the results of being born Black in a white-oriented world. Now, I am

50

certainly not asking anyone to feel sorry for me or to create conditions where I can be secure in my own sorrow. I realize that everyone has problems and most are far worse than mine. One of the processes that has served me well over the years is to determine the source of the problem, as well as, the part I play in it, then deal with it. So, the essay, "Why was I born Black?" has served to determine the source of the problem, confront it, and then create an understanding that will serve me.

The Dunbar Keynote address deals with an issue of "ego." That is, "How could I effectively show my peers, my teachers, and friends what I've done with my life?" First, there is a strong lineage of Black High Schools that preceded integration. High schools like mine all over the south produced most of the highly successful Black people of that time even though they existed under the conditions of segregation. When I tell many of the people I've met that I was the boatswain in my high school production of the operetta, H.M.S. Pinafore by Gilbert and Sullivan, played French horn, as well as described the course work I took in chemistry, physics, music, and math, many of these people are surprised. I graduated from the largest black High School in Arkansas with a history of highly successful, productive, and proud people.

Because of the coming onset of integration, among other factors, Dunbar High School was changed to a junior high school and a new high school was built. The new high school of course was named after a white Educator, Horace Mann. Sometimes in the 1970s, a board was created that was composed of former Dunbar High School students. It was decided to have a reunion of the students who attended Dunbar from 1927 to 1956. The reunion is held every two years somewhere in the U.S. since most of the graduates are spread all over the country. My aunt, Anna Evelyn Burch, was on the board of directors and decided I should be the Keynote Speaker for the 1995 reunion that was held in Detroit, Michigan. There was some controversy about my selection, so I knew my presentation had to be beyond reproach. During my career as a trainer/consultant my hardest audiences have been all-Black participants. It is a far more competitive and difficult environment; no room for mistakes.

I worked harder on that presentation than any I ever made. More so than the presentation I made before a national audience of the Society of Petroleum Engineers in Los Angles in 1968. I wrote twelve drafts and practiced at least 24 times out loud. The resulting presentation was one of the most rewarding experiences I've ever had.

Although my message may be different and challenging, it is based on the choices I've made. Sometimes I feel sad that I didn't stay on the normal path that most of my classmates took. I opted out of that reality because I knew that this new reality had far more interesting and rewarding possibilities.

These essays, then, offer an opportunity to demonstrate the perspectives and perceptions that lead to the development of the "Synthesis of Thomas III". The Dunbar Speech was also a report on the state of affairs in the "Synthesis of Thomas III".

The Emperor's New Clothes Revisited (1988)

How often have you been influenced by someone else without confirming the validity of their ideas? Much of what we believe today we have accepted unconsciously. In other words, we have bought into the idea or concept without determining whether or not it was valid. Our parents, churches, schools, friends, and government have all been indoctrinated; each one of us. I am not saying that everything you have been told is a lie or untrue. I am saying you may need to determine for yourself the validity of a statement, ideas or so called facts.

Many so-called ideas or facts like the history of your area can be different in one place or another. For instance, you might have been born in another part of town and therefore be in a different socioeconomic status. You might have gone to a different set of schools and have different allegiances in sports. You also might have gone to a different church and therefore belong to a different religious group. You might have a different set of friends. You could have been borne in a different country and therefore speak a different language, hate this country, eat different foods and have your marriage arranged by your parents.

Most of us are asleep, that is, we accept most things in life unconsciously without asking, is there a different way of life that's better for me. I believe that it is time to wake up; it is time to say, "You're naked", and live the life you really want. So, how can we make this change and challenge what we "know" to be true. If you think it time, then read on.

Most of us have read at one time or another, Hans Christian Anderson's story for children, "The Emperor's New Clothes". This classic story became one of my favorites as an adult when I began to analyze the events of life. One meaning that can be derived from the story is, we can program ourselves or be programmed under the right conditions to believe anything. That is, when we want something badly enough, another individual can appeal to our vanity or our need and as a result, con us into thinking they can give it to us. This story certainly has meaning for us today!

Well now, the Emperor, with his vain self, decided he wanted something that was better than and different from anything in existence. So, two enterprising tailors decided to devise a scheme to take advantage of the Emperor's desperate need. They went to the Emperor and told him that they had found a way to make the most fantastic set of clothes that had ever been made. "There was one catch," they told the Emperor, "these clothes are so special that imbeciles and incompetent people cannot see them."

Now you all know the story. The Emperor was concerned that something was up, so he sent his top staff members, one by one, to check on the clothes. Of course, not one staff member saw anything and since they didn't want to appear stupid or incompetent, they began to "see" something. By the time the Emperor went to see the clothes for himself, he had been told by all his staff members how fantastic these clothes were. When he looked at the "clothes," he didn't see anything either but he didn't want to look stupid in front of all his staff and tailors. And furthermore, since he certainly didn't want to appear incompetent, he became hypnotized by his own command and beliefs.

The Emperor in all his imagined magnificence marched in a parade; to show his subjects how good he looked. His subjects, of course didn't see anything but since they didn't want to feel stupid or incompetent, they began to rave about his fine clothes. This went on, until a small kid said, "He's naked!"

How do we make sense of the above story? As we analyze this story, we find first that we all, like the Emperor, have wants, needs, and desires. Sometimes these wants, needs, and desires are overwhelming and, in some cases, they become addictive. Second, there are people, the con artists, who seek to fulfill their own wants and desires by taking advantage of us. Third, there are people who get used and serve as a vehicle to fulfill the needs of others. Fourth, there are people, like the little child, who shout aloud or just say to them, he's naked!

What really makes this story work, the magic ingredient as it were is the condition set by the con artists, the unscrupulous tailors. People didn't admit they didn't see the clothes because they did not want to seem stupid and incompetent. This type of condition sets up a dilemma or conflict. This conflict works best when it threatens our survival or well-being. By setting up these conflicts, people can be fooled or tricked into accepting things, events, or information they wouldn't otherwise accept. On the political scene, this device is used on a regular basis.

How does this story relate to us today? A theme or subtitle for this article might be "Whose Reality or What Reality Am I, You..We Going to CHOOSE?"

I believe that most people don't make conscious choices. We live life by default: We react to situations and events unconsciously. We become like the emperor, where addictive-like wants and desires can be installed because we have bought into the "Madison Avenue Advertising" approach to the so-called good life. Then, someone comes along and says - very subtlety, of course - "I can get you these things, but are you willing to pay the price?" In most cases, they won't tell us what the real price, that is, the hidden charges. When we want something too badly, sometimes we usually don't investigate the consequences of accepting these things, one way or the other.

No one shouts, "You're Naked!"

We want liberty and the pursuit of happiness. We fight for these things over and over again. Then someone comes along and says, "This is the way it is supposed to be. This is what you need and, if you don't accept it that way or respond accordingly, you're not being an American, a good citizen, etc." So we adopt their notion of what an American or good citizen is without investigating the consequences.

No one shouts, "You're Naked!"

We also want to show how good we are and make a good impression. So, we send our best and our brightest to other communities to prove that we are as good as anyone, again, without investigating the consequences of our actions.

And, no one shouts, "You're Naked!" Or, maybe we hear it, but like the Emperor, decide to continue on any way because we don't want to be embarrassed.

Today there are many things about which we can cry, "You're Naked!" such as, our physical well-being, nutrition, lifestyle, emotions, and political awareness. If we desire to take control of our lives and eliminate the default habits, it's time to shout, "You're Naked!" Then, we can begin to make Conscious - Deliberate - Choices about how we think, act, or make decisions. To do so means determining and understanding the consequences of our actions by asking questions such as: Who influences me or how am I being influenced? Are conflicts being setup that put me in a dilemma? Am I being tricked into doing something I really don't want to do or deal with?

A second set of questions we might ask are, "What are my alternatives? And, what will happen if I do chose a given alternative? And, what would happen if I don't?" By answering these questions, we can determine how we can resolve the situation or issue with the least amount of stress and the greatest amount of satisfaction.

Now you might ask, "How can this method of questioning be put into practice?" The nomination of Judge Thomas as a Supreme Court Justice of the United States offers a good example. First of all, we, as Black people, were trumped and found ourselves in a dilemma. Should we support someone who is Black with whom we may frequently not agree or should we recommend that he not be confirmed and therefore not support someone who is Black for such a high office.

We found ourselves in a very complicated situation. However, it might help us by remembering that we are very different from the Blacks of the fifties and sixties. We do not represent a homogeneous population anymore, if we did then. We have become much more sophisticated and at the same time more differentiated. Furthermore, we need individuals who can mix with different groups and deal with broad issues so that we don't get taken for granted. We have an agenda that needs the cooperation of many elements within our society.

Now that Judge Thomas has been nominated we have to deal with the consequences of supporting him or not supporting him. You may not agree with Judge Thomas's frame of reference, however, he is **Black As He Defines It**! And so you might ask, "Will his frame of reference be better than that of any other individual President Bush is likely to appoint if Judge Thomas is not confirmed. In all likelihood, the next person won't be Black. There are other Blacks who may be more to your or my liking. However, these Blacks are not going to be considered.

We must also remember that George Bush was elected (you may not have voted for him) as our President. Furthermore, He's going to be in office two more years, and four extra years after that unless we make a new choice for President. And since we elected him, we must accept the consequences of that election. President Bush is not going to appoint another person like Justice Thurgood Marshall. He is going to appoint someone who is conservative.

There is another consideration. Believe it or not, time heals many wounds. History shows us that many times a Supreme Court Justice, after being in office for a while, changes and leans more toward the middle away from either the liberal or conservative extremes. So, patience may be in order.

The Judge Thomas confirmation is an excellent example of the Emperor's New Clothes. We can get caught up in the rhetoric and emotions, and thus deal with his confirmation by default. Or, we can ask questions which deal with the many frames of reference. One question is the issue of quotas. Are we trying to show that we won't vote for someone just because he or she is not Black enough? Should Blacks have one voice? Who is going to define who we are? Do we want to lose the Black representation and reference at that level?

57

These are only some of the questions we might ask. It's hard to see the forest for the trees. If we believe everything we see, hear, or otherwise experience about someone without understanding what the consequences of adopting these beliefs are, we are bending over and asking to be kicked!

Decide to make a Conscious - Deliberate - Choice for yourself. Who's going to shout! He's Naked! Think about the consequences surrounding the possible choices you have, and then decide. Then, whatever you decide is best for you.

So, what do you think?

One of the main slogans in the "Synthesis of Thomas III," is to "Make Conscious, Deliberate, Choices." "Making Conscious, Deliberate, Choices" is easy when things are going your way. However, when things are not going your way or when it appears that all the choices available are against you or not in your best interest, it is best to choose anyway. "Making a Conscious, Deliberate, Choice" at this time, takes away or at least reduces the sting and at the same time empowers you.

Clarence Thomas was elected to and is currently a justice in the Supreme Court.

Why Was I Born Black? (1989)

Why am I Black? That's a very complicated question to answer. The proper question is, "Why was I born Black?" I shall answer this question in terms of its spiritual, historical, and social significance.

During my younger years, I was consumed by the need to know why things were as they were. Why Negroes were always treated as though we were less than human? Why did Negroes always have to defer to whites? Why didn't Negroes have the same opportunities as whites? Why was everything that was wholesome, including God and Jesus, defined in terms of white people? If the United States was a free country, then why weren't Negroes free? Like a little kid, WHY? WHY? WHY?

As a consequence of growing up under these conditions it became very difficult to deal with life. There were no answers to these questions, at least none that satisfied me. There was nothing in the history books, nothing in the newspaper, or at the movies that gave me hope of answers. For years, there was no past, no present, and no future that showed anything worthwhile. As a result, I had no positive feelings about being a Negro. And, I was so sold on this perception that I was not open to any possibilities. For instance, I had the opportunity to take a Negro history course in high school. My reply was, "What for? What have we done?"

It took me fifty years to gather the information needed to answer these questions. That information is used as the basis for this article.

Spiritual

I believe that the foundation and maintenance of my being emanates from a spiritual reference. It is my belief that we are here to recognize and nurture our oneness with God. We are already one with God; however, we have lost that awareness--as represented by the "Fall of Man." It is my belief that we are more than just physical beings. The most important element of our being, our essence is, immortal, infinite, and universal. This essence, not the physical self, was created in the image of God and therefore represents our oneness.

In pursuit of the awareness of this oneness, we chose to become a physical being on this earth. In doing so, we chose our parents as well as the place or community we were born into. The choice of our parents and community dictates our socioeconomic status through adolescence and the type of formative experiences we will have. Overcoming the problems caused by these experiences helps us to grow and mature, thereby, increases our ability to consciously recognize this oneness.

I believe we chose to be born on this planet under varying conditions which to each one of us may seem like the pits at times, or for some, most of the time. Every one of us has problems that we must overcome. The best way I know to overcome these problems is to live and breathe God's love as taught by Jesus and other great masters. I believe that God gave love and provided the means to regain oneness to all peoples on this planet. No one or group has the inside track. One way to consciously achieve this oneness that all religions teach is to look inside our hearts.

I firmly believe that we are all part of God's consciousness and therefore will return one day to that consciousness. How long it takes for each one of us to realize this oneness depends on how long it takes for each of us to fully realize God's love and power. It's like the old Fram commercial on TV; you can pay $3.95 for a filter now or wait until later and pay $3950 for a new engine (pay me now or pay me later). I'm going for oneness now.

Historical

History is a reference to selected events and people that have been assigned importance by the narrator. There are literally millions of events and people at any given point in time. Someone has to determine which of these events and people are ones that have the most impact on the course of events. So history has to be read with the understanding that it is written from the perspective of the narrator. In this world, history is written in the eyes of the victor or conqueror.

The way history has been taught in our country, it is hard to believe that any minority group has made significant contributions to the development of our country. The contributions made by minorities have had limited space in the history books. We have special weeks or periods during the year to honor and supplement these contributions. In order to find the wealth of information, not found in textbooks, magazines, newspapers, journals, etc., individuals must conduct this research on their own.

I began my own study of history twenty years ago. And, as I obtained results from this study, I began to understand that I do fit in. Blacks, as well as, other minority groups have made significant contributions to this country and the world that affect all areas of life, physically, mentally, emotionally, and spiritually, not just to music or sports. I've discovered that much of western scientific, religious, and spiritual knowledge has its origins from Black (Egyptian), Native American and Indian (India) civilizations.

At 45, I finally matured with the recognition that Blacks have had a significant part in history. Thus, my anger with whites began to abate. Blacks, like all racial groups have had and will have their dominant periods. Dominant periods change with time. I discovered that we must first recognize that change is the one constant we all must submit to. "Everything must change, nothing stays the same," is the only constant.

I once asked a student of mine how long have whites been in control of the world. Her answer was, of course, "always." The real answer is closer to 300 years. We have the illusion that whites have been in control all of the time because they control the history books. Therefore, when we read history books or watch movies about the past or future, we can be drawn into the illusion that whites always have been and always will be in control.

I also asked this student, what is the first wonder of the world? And so, I also ask you the reader, "what is the best known, if not first, wonder of the world?" Your answer most likely will be, "The Pyramids of Egypt!" As you answer, you might ask, "Why is the first or best known wonder of the world, a Black monument?" If you have any question as to whether or not that Black people made the Pyramids, look at your history books and turn to the Egyptian pictures and statures of Pharaohs.

I wish I could show in this article pictures from the Ramses exhibit. The Ramses Exhibit was held in Dallas and other cities in 1987. If you weren't able to attend, you can read articles related to the exhibit as printed in the *Dallas Times Herald*, November 1, 1987 or the Dallas Life Magazine on February 26, 1989 (check them out!). These articles and exhibits show unmistakable proof that ancient peoples and rulers of ancient Egypt were Black. In order words, the first, and one of the greatest and longest continuous civilizations (over 3000 years) in the Western world, was created and run by Black people.

Through the use of motion pictures, ancient Egyptians were shown to be white. Other Black civilizations, such as, Merowe, Ghana, Mali, Songhai, etc., have been documented but were not known to the public. A grand illusion was created that depicted Blacks as inferior and whites as superior to all.

The point to be made here is that Black people have had their place in the sun and will have it again. It took Europeans 1000 years to shed the yoke of the Roman Empire and yet it was the common thread of language and enculturation that helped to create the industrial revolution and scientific progress. Black people have been out of slavery for a little more than 120 years, so in some ways we are way ahead of schedule. So, let's create our own destiny along with whites and other peoples on this planet.

Social

We have been socialized and therefore hypnotized into accepting realities that are not favorable to Blacks. We have taken on a set of beliefs, and given a post hypnotic command that if we challenge that belief we are un-American, unfair, and even discriminating.

We have been taught to give up our birthright, by a wholesale acceptance of the white version of the American Dream. We have accepted their basis of religious, educational, scientific, and educational practices as being the only way to be. We have to accept their version of the way to live as the standard to judge civilization. We have accepted whites as our jailers and have asked them to free us.

Freedom, regaining our birthright, and setting our own standard does not begin with being set free. It begins by freeing ourselves, re-establishing our own birthright from within, and creating standards that will reflect the true meaning of the American Declaration of Independence and the Constitution. It starts in each individual's mind and heart.

When you don't like yourself, it's hard to create a wholesome reality. And when you don't even realize you don't like yourself it becomes almost impossible. Many of us, Black, white, or otherwise don't like ourselves. To change the conditions of our lives, we have to not only understand but also make an active effort to change that perspective.

It's hard to love someone else if you don't love and respect yourself. Loving yourself begins by letting go of the shackles of fear, self-hated, and the illusions created by others. Whites cannot free us nor can anybody else free us. We must free ourselves. To free ourselves we must define who we are, what we are, and how we are going to make it in the world.

Freeing us starts by finding an inner peace though God's love that can be described as an inner flame that never flickers. By doing so, we can live in harmony with ourselves, other Blacks (before we exterminate ourselves), and whites and other races.

So, Why Was I Born Black?

Being born Black in this time period has given me an opportunity to learn, grow, and transform into a God-centered being. This transformation has gone from anger and hated to love, to a realization of oneness with myself, other Blacks, all races of peoples and things in the universe. I can truly take my place among Blacks, whites and everyone else. Being born Black in this time period has presented me with a perfect way to understand that it doesn't really matter what color you are, who or what you are, or how much you have or don't have.

I am now totally proud of my race, heritage, and birthright. No one will ever define who I am again. No longer am I subconsciously directed by fear or self-hatred. No longer am I making decisions or acting by default. I still have problems, as much as anyone. However, I am now making "CONSCIOUS, DELIBERATE, CHOICES" to resolve these problems, and other issues in my life. I can share my life harmoniously with my family, friends, and all peoples: Blacks, whites, and others. As a result, I am free to be all that I can be. I'm still working on being one with God consciously! What more can anyone ask for?

This essay demonstrates my quest to establish my own identity and was quite liberating. It signifies my acceptance of me as person and thus became a very important step in developing "The Synthesis of Thomas III."

Dunbar Keynote Speech
"Scholarship - The Tradition Then And Now"
Scholarship: To Be Or .. Not! (1995)

Introduction

Before I begin this speech, I would like to tell you three stories that will set the stage for the information I want to share with you today. They are:

The Three Wise Persons

Three Wise Persons, a Western, Eastern, and Southern Wise Person were fishing from a boat in a lake. After some time, the Eastern Wise Person said, "I'm thirsty," and he stepped out of the boat, and walked across the water to the shore and got something to drink. He, then, walked back across the water got back into the boat and sat down.

The Western Wise Person was shocked, he had heard and read about events such as this, and here he was experiencing a seemingly miracle right before his eyes.

Pretty soon, the Southern Wise Person said, "I'm hungry!" and she stepped out of the boat, and walked across the water to the shore and got something to eat. She then walked back across the water, got back into the boat and sat down.

The Western Wise person was beside himself, this was too much!

After a while, the Western Wise Person had to use the bathroom. Not to be outdone, he stepped out of the boat into the water, and promptly, went 10 feet under.

The Eastern Wise person said to the Southern Wise person, "Shall we tell him where the stumps are?"

Mulla Nasrudin, The Fool

Mulla Nasrudin is a character in Sufi Tales. He represents a range of characters from a wise man to a fool.

One day, Mulla Nasrudin was on his knees in front of his house. He appeared to be searching for something. A friend came and said, "Mulla Nasrudin, what are you doing?"

Mulla Nasrudin replied, "I'm looking for my keys."

His friend said, "May I help you?"

Mulla Nasrudin replied, "Yes!" and the two searched for Mulla Nasrudin's keys.

After a while, 30 minutes or more, the friend asked, Mulla Nasrudin, "Are you sure you lost your key here? We have been looking for some time and haven't found your keys."

Mulla Nasrudin told his friend, "I didn't lose them out here. I lost them in the house!"

His friend said, "Then, why are you looking out here?"

Mulla Nasrudin told his friend, "It's light out here!"

The Young Man On The Path

One day a young man was walking along a path along a mountainside with steep drop-offs. After walking for some time, he lost his footing and fell off a ridge. About 20 feet down, he grabbed a hold of a branch that was there. He hung on for dear life, as there was a 1000-foot drop along rocks and boulders, below.

The young man shouted, "Help! Help! Is anybody up there?"

He waited and shouted again, "Help! Help! Is anybody up there?"

Then he heard a Voice, out of the clear blue sky, which said, "Yes, I am here and I will help you. I will help you only if you believe."

The young man shouted, passionately, "I believe, I believe!"

The Voice said, "If you believe, let go of that limb."

The young man looked up to the 20 feet of space between him and the top of the ridge, then, he looked down to the 1000 feet of rocks and boulders below, and said, "Is anybody else out there!"

These three stories personify the message I bring to you today. We need to understand where the stumps are that define our path. We need to know where to look in order to find where the real treasure is located within us. And finally, we need to trust and have faith that we will be guided to our goal.

Three stories present us then, with three basic ideas:

The Three Wise Person, Western, Eastern, & Southern:

Knowing the Path

Mulla Nasrudin, the Fool and his car keys:

Knowing where to Look

The Young Man on the Path:

Having Faith

Members of the Dais, the National Dunbar Alumni Association Board of Directors and fellow Alumnae of Dunbar Sr. High School and friends; I want to particularly pay my respects to my aunt, Ms. Anna Evelyn Burch, a member of the Board, who recommended me for this speech, and finally pay respects to my Mother and Father, Evie Jean and Thomas J. Nolan, Jr. They are the reason I am here.

The title of my speech is, "Scholarship: To Be or .. NOT! It is derived from the theme of this program today, "Scholarship - The Tradition Then and Now."

SCHOLARSHIP – THE TRADITION THEN AND NOW: SCHOLARSHIP: TO BE OR .. NOT!

The Text

The title of this speech was chosen because it expresses how some of our kids deal with the concept of scholarship. **Not!** is one of their favorite phrases. Many kids in our schools have this view that scholarship is <u>not</u> desired; it's to be abhorred. The goal of this speech is to discuss my vision of scholarship, and introduce two different perspectives that can be integrated into the lives of our kids. Therefore, this speech is dedicated to our children; they are our future.

A Scholar is defined, according to the American Heritage Dictionary, as "a learned or erudite person; a specialist in a given branch of the humanities." Scholarship" is further defined by the same book, as "the methods, discipline, and attainment of a scholar; and as knowledge resulting from study and research in a particular field." In scholastic terms, I have just given you a formal definition.

Now, classically, when we think of scholarship, we think of a scholar who seeks to understand fully the basis or foundation of an idea, where it comes from; what it is doing, and where it is going. A scholar seeks to get a full understanding or knowledge of the material or idea at hand. To me, this knowledge comes in four stages, (1) experience, (2) understanding, (3) explanation, and (4) application. That is, you have an experience, (but just because you've had the experience, doesn't mean that you understand what's happening); therefore, you must process the experience and after some processing period, you reach a level of understanding; however, you may understand something and yet, have trouble explaining it), then, after further processing, you are able to explain the experience to someone else; but you can explain something to someone without knowing how to use or apply it), after even more processing, then, you are able to apply the experience to some problem or situation. Knowledge, ultimately is, that which is borne of experience, understanding, explanation, and application.

However, I want to present a different definition, that is, my personal definition of scholarship. I'd like to define scholarship in terms of a focus, an undying focus on some goal or task to accomplish whatever you want. In other words, a focus that is so strong that you don't allow anyone or anything to take you away from the attainment of your goal. It doesn't matter whether you are in the sciences, arts, academic circles, athletics, management or any other area you would like to deal with.

I am going to argue that we need both definitions of scholarship. Our children need both definitions to increase their probability of success in life and it's up to parents, the community, as well as the schools to teach them. I would like, then, to show you first, the importance of the traditional concept of scholarship for Black Americans; and second, the value both personally and professionally my personal concept of scholarship has for every aspect of our daily life. And, I want to show how vital it is that we find the ways and means to persuade our children and grandchildren of the importance of scholarship. This is too big a job to just delegate to the schools.

The first perspective, the traditional concept of scholarship, allows us to address the difficulties that arise when we do not place an emphasis on scholars and scholarship. Without an emphasis on scholarship, we won't have enough people to manage the worlds of science, commerce, management, etc. But, just as importantly, we won't have enough people who are able to do the research, classification, or set standards to define for ourselves who we are, where we come from, and where we might go. Without an emphasis on scholarship we will continue to be bombarded by books like "The Bell Curve" by Herrnstein and Murray (the highly controversial book that seeks to validate many of the current stereotypes about intellectual capabilities and social values of Blacks).

Now, let us look at who defines us. When I attended Dunbar in senior high school, I had an opportunity to take Negro History and

69

I recall saying to myself, "What for? What have we done?" Since our history wasn't a part of the regular curriculum, it held no legitimacy for me. There were no visible comparisons or evidence that made it important and it was not taught in the regular curriculum. I just didn't have any idea of who we were as a people, and it didn't matter. I was well in my twenties before I began to explore our past.

Years later, I did start searching and finally found what I was looking for as I developed the prospectus for my dissertation during the late seventies. I spent several years, studying how our history relates to the development of Eastern and Western Civilizations. My training in research assisted me in finding the information I needed. It was out there but I had to dig deeply to find it.

There was little evidence around me as a young student that gave me information about how we fit in. In fact, the discovery process was very painful, and I became really angry. The discovery started when a friend gave me a book about the empires of the west coast nations of Africa. It was a primer and a very simple and easy book to read but it sparked my interest and initiated a study of history that wasn't satisfied until I completed the background information for my dissertation work in 1979. I found we have a rich heritage, in fact, all peoples do.

I not only discovered information about the most ancient and famous 3000 year old cultures of Egypt, but learned that there were many other African Cultures that had glorious histories, too, such as, Merowe, Zimbabwe, Ghana, Mali, and Songhai to name a few.

I've asked audiences and you might ask yourselves, how long have Whites been in control of the world? If you said, more that 200 to 300 years you would be wrong! Most Whites, as well as some of us, usually say since the beginning of time. It's only been 200 to 300 years out of 6000 years of recorded history.

All through history, nations have conquered each other, power has moved from place to place, race to race, and group to group.

Even in Europe, we can talk about the conquest of southern Europe by Hannibal, in the 3rd century. Also some parts of Europe was over run once by Attila the Hun and twice by the Mongols (Genghis Khan and his sons) before the 13th century. Many of the ethnic problems that exist in Eastern Europe today stem from these conquests. Most importantly, its renaissance was initiated as a result of influence of the Moors that conquered Spain. So, even Europe has been under the influence of outsiders during its modern history.

And then, I learned about the contributions we have made to this country. John Batiste du Sable established the first site that led to the development of the city of Chicago, Benjamin Banneker helped develop the plans for Washington, DC and developed the first American clock, even though he had never seen one; Dr. Charles R. Drew was instrumental in developing blood plasma processing, storage and transfusion therapy and founded the blood bank; George Washington Carver, developed multiple uses for the peanut and the rotation of crops to regenerate the soil. These people represent just the tip of the iceberg of contributions to this country. Although the specific number of achievements by Blacks discussed in school history books has increased, history is still taught almost exclusively from a European perspective, it does not include an Afrocentric or multicultural perspective. The Afrocentric perspective anchors Black students with historical factors that they can relate to. In order to get this perspective, Black students must still go outside the system. What we do get, are bestsellers, editorials, and news stories that publish or support unsavory perceptions about us.

Three excellent books that attack a wide spectrum of misconceptions explaining, how this whole process of misleading information got started in the first place, and how we might initiate change are as follows:

Don't Believe the Hype by Farai Chideya

Yurugu: An African Centered Critique of European Cultural Thought and Behavior by Marimba Ani

71

Race Matters by Cornel West

Chideya challenges the current misperceptions about the number of Black men in prison vs. college, the number of single Black women on welfare, and the incidence of drug use among Blacks as compared with Whites. She sets the record straight. Research as well as history is a function of those who perform or write it.

Ani presents a scholarly treatise on the development of behaviors and thought patterns of Europeans as it relates to Black Americans. It's tough reading; she documents everything, leaving little room for error.

West in his book, Race Matters, admonishes our failure to intervene in public affairs when it's not convenient for us to do so. We need to exercise the right to disagree in public. We don't all think alike. We are a more diverse people now and we need to deal with the world from these different perspectives.

We need more scholars like West, Ani, and Chideya to name a few, who challenge the status quo, who use the traditional perspective to show the side that recorded history fails to show. These authors show us how this society seeks to control our minds. So, unless we decide to deal with these issues as a whole, and take responsibility for making this information known to our kids, who will do it for us or after we are gone?

Schools have made many improvements in recent years by including Blacks and other minorities within the teaching curriculum. Television and movies have increasingly given us more favorable and challenging roles, although there are still many inconsistencies and biases when it comes to reporting about how we live, work, and play. We need more Afrocentric curricula, news columns, television and movie roles that will inspire us to greater heights. As more Black scholars are available, it will become easier to integrate an Afrocentric point of view in school curricula, the media, etc. Or we can do it on our own.

The American Society is becoming more and more technically oriented each day. Without the proper skills, knowledge, and attitude, too many of our kids will be left behind. In other words, all of our kids need to be scholastically oriented in order to be successful. Some of our kids are saying to their peers who are trying to be scholastically oriented, why are you trying to be like "them", why can't you be more like us?

The scholastic orientation should be <u>desired</u> and therefore the <u>norm</u>. We need to persuade kids who don't do well and/or don't want to do well, to want to be more like the scholastically oriented kids. One of the reasons kids don't accept the scholastic orientation, may be, that they don't feel it's applicable to them and don't see its practical applications. We need to show them; therefore, ways in which scholarship can work for them, the ways in which it can be relevant for their lives. Teaching them history from an Afrocentric perspective is a crucial tool toward accomplishing this goal.

According to my personal definition of scholarship, the second perspective of this speech, a scholar is not only a textbook student but also one who is able to apply his or her focus toward some goal, blocking out all distractions; a Michael Jordan or Leontyne Price for instance. When Michael is Air Jordan, he probably has no idea what is going on around him. There is only the ball, the basket and the people he's dealing with. When Leontyne Price sings the role of Leonora in Verdi's IL Trovatore, she probably loses all perspective of herself and becomes Leonora. Studies have shown that the ability to focus on their goals, blocking out all distractions is consistent among most great athletes and performers. When Michael and Ms. Price lose themselves in their art, they find a peace like no other; they become balanced and centered. Focus may also, then be described in terms of being balanced and centered. So, I'd like to talk about how kids can use this focus to obtain a sense of balance and centeredness. It is not just limited to the stars!

One of my former students, who was raised in the Detroit area, was part of a group I organized while teaching at Langston University. He became a minister after college. His name is Michael Milbern. He was the Graduation Speaker for one of the local high school districts in the early eighties. During this speech he gave three essential things that one needs to achieve success: A Faith in God; Belief in Self; and, a Plan. I have redefined these three components, integrated them with the concept of focus and called them "Articles of Being." I further propose that the "Articles of Being" can be used to develop and maintain a sense of balance and centeredness.

One of the problems I have identified as the basis for trouble in the schools is that in addition to a disdain for traditional view of scholarship, many of our kids do not have a faith in God (I mean more than paying lip service), they don't believe in themselves and they certainly don't have a plan. I would like to use the "Articles of Being," to show you how to help them develop and maintain a sense of balance and centeredness.

I doubt that Michael and Leontyne Price only recently discovered they had a strong focus. They developed their strong focus through practice and hard work. We all know people who have or had talent, maybe greater than Michael or Ms. Price. They were not successful because they were not able to develop and put in the hard work it takes to maintain the focus to apply that talent. A strong focus then, is not limited to a few people who excel in the sciences, literature, and other areas. Everyone has the potential to maximize their God given talents. Most of us just don't know how.

How, then, can we help our children apply this strong focus and thus, achieve a sense of balance and centeredness? Focus is defined by the American Heritage Dictionary as, "An adjustment for distinctness or clarity; to concentrate: *as in focused all his attention on finding a solution.*"

Since we are discussing scholarship as a means to success, I would also like to define success. I chose to describe highly successful people as those who are prosperous, happy, and have found peace of mind. Money and/or fame are not the secret in themselves, otherwise the rich and famous would have the most satisfying lives. Many famous and/or rich people experience miserable lives because they lack the centeredness and balance to go with their focus. One of the best ways to develop this complete focus is to utilize the three components of the "Articles of Being:" A Faith in God; A Belief in Self; and a Plan.

Faith

Now, in order to describe a Faith in God concept, I like to explain it in terms of the first three components of the 12 Step Substance Abuse Program. That is, (1) recognizing that you can't solve life's problems by yourself; (2) recognizing that there is a power higher than you, and that you must accept or surrender to this power, and (3) asking that power to help you deal with life's problems.

When times are bad or difficult, most of us will profess a faith in God. We must however, have a Faith that is ongoing. I asked myself once, and you might do it, too, "Do I Believe in God?" I mean I really challenged myself. I did ask and an answer came about three months later.. THAT I DID, and at that point I consciously accepted my connection with GOD!

Faith in God, then, occurs when you accept or surrender to your connection with God. It is the most important thing you can do. Therefore, you not only seek to connect with God no matter what the circumstances are, but maintain that connection at all times. When you are not feeling that connection, you are in trouble. Without that foundation, you might as well forget everything else and just hang it up. We as a people know this on one level, but sometimes, we forget. Our faith drops to a subconscious level; we need to keep it on a conscious level, where it is available to us.

Belief

How about a belief in Self? We can all say we believe in ourselves, but do we really? There are times when belief in self is strong. However, there are those unconscious waves or patterns that can force or cause us to limit ourselves or actually let go of that belief. We each have to find out the source of these patterns. What are the things or events that activate the patterns that limit belief in self? In the past, the times when you experienced the most difficulty, you will find patterns you created that activated these limits. These patterns can be traced back to beliefs that don't serve us. When I was younger, I tried to find someone who really loved me so I could love myself. Well, it did not work.

My mother taught and instilled within me, just be Thomas! It was a very tall order. My father taught me perseverance. I was 35 when I discovered I had a problem. I created an image I thought everyone would like, rather than be myself. Well, it took another ten years to learn how to be Thomas. Now, for ten years, I have been growing in the understanding of who Thomas is.

Then, one day, I discovered what I longed for was already there. Through my conscious connection with God, I realized the true meaning of love. When I allowed myself to experience that love, I no longer needed someone outside of me to make me feel loved. And, since I didn't need something outside of me to make me feel loved, I could love and be loved by someone else.

Plan
Do you know how to get what you want? Too many of us are stuck in life and don't know how to create what we want without causing us harm or difficulties. In order to get what you want, you must deal with three things. One, Clarity, you must be clear about what you want, that is, really know what you want. Two, Energy, you must have enough energy to create what you want. The only way to have the energy needed to create what you want is to connect with God on a daily basis. And, three Sabotage, you must understand how to discover the patterns you use to sabotage yourself.

Now, Clarity can be obtained by first embracing the beliefs that you can get anything you want. Then, adopt the attitude that there are no limitations, no barriers, nothing to stop you from getting what you want. For instance, go back in time and look at what you did when you accomplished what you really wanted. The things we really want and have passion behind it, we usually get. You already have then, an established process that works and can you use this process consciously.

Energy is obtained by connecting with God consciously on a regular basis through prayer or meditation. I make a distinction between those prayers we use to ask for something, and the prayers that allow us to connect with God. To me, if you haven't connected, there's no use in your asking. I call connecting prayers, meditation. Connecting with God on a regular basis helps us to create or get what we want.

Sabotage is a function of the patterns or mindsets we adopt to correct situations when things don't go our way. Sometimes they are patterns that we install to solve problems or situations. When these situations are resolved we no longer need them. However, if we forget to erase or restructure them for future use, these patterns can work against us. Other people who tried to control us may have also installed patterns within us. They are able to install these patterns within us, by getting us to feel judgments, blame, guilt, or shame. Learn just to say **NO!** or **NOT!** So, say **NO!** to judgments..**NO!** to Blame,..**NO!** to Guilt,..**NO!** to Shame.

When I want something, I use the following procedure, (1) gain clarity; (2) make sure I am and have been connecting with God on a regular basis, and (3) go into a special prayer of asking and **ASK**,,,,It is written, "Ask And You Shall Receive". After I have made my request, I ask for confirmation, and then listen to determine if indeed it's okay. If I'm about to sabotage myself, I will not only be notified but I will receive advice about how I can remove the sabotage, as well. When my answer is affirmative, I Let Go and Let God!

I have given you an overview of two perspectives of scholarship. Perspective one is to be applied by the individual for the benefit and continuation of our community: locally, nationally, and internationally. Perspective two is to be applied by the individual, specifically for our kids, as the basic survival tools for their future well-being, something that they can use and enjoy. I have been introducing this view of scholarship in Student Leadership Training Programs to kids in Oklahoma, for the past twelve years. I invite you to do the same.

I would like to end the presentation with three stories, The Wiz, Chocolate Brown and the Seven Dwarfs, and Row, Row, Row Your Boat.

The Wiz!

Most of you have heard of the movie, "Wizard of Oz." I, however, prefer the remake of this movie made in the late 70's, the Wiz. At any rate, the Wiz essentially has four characters. First there is Dorothy, who doesn't fully understand her capabilities and three other characters that act as surrogate personalities for her, including the Scarecrow, the Tin Man, and the Lion. The Scarecrow needs a brain, the Tin Man, a heart, and the Lion, courage. In other words, if Dorothy is to know herself, she must know how to utilize her brain, that is, her brain has multiple sections. The most important section to Dorothy is the cerebral cortex that has two distinct components, called the left-brain and right-brain. Each of these brains has its own function, with the left-brain having a logical, sequential orientation and the right brain having a patterned, gestalt orientation. For Dorothy, it is not a matter of which brain to use but to have the ability to use both in coordination with each other, i.e., having a balance between the two.

The Tin Man represents Dorothy's need to mediate her actions by accessing her feelings. When Dorothy is using feelings as a guide, she is being guided by an inner strength that will always help her make the best decision at any time. Once Dorothy knows what direction she wants to take, she must to have the courage to take each step in that direction to reach her goals. When all three components are clicking and working together, then Dorothy not only knows what she wants, she knows how to get there, and has the strength to make it.

Chocolate Brown and the Seven Dwarfs

Have you heard of Chocolate Brown and the Seven Dwarfs? You haven't? What do you mean you haven't heard of Chocolate Brown and the Seven Dwarfs? Oh! I forgot! You call it, "Snow

White and the Seven Dwarfs!" But this is my story and I shall call it what I want to. Anyway, Chocolate Brown was the most beautiful woman in the world. However, the Queen thought she was the most beautiful. When she learned that Chocolate Brown was the most beautiful, she did everything she could to become the most beautiful. She even tried to have Chocolate Brown killed but was unsuccessful. So, she disguised herself as an old hag and tricked Chocolate Brown into eating a poisoned apple. Chocolate Brown ate it and fell into a deep sleep. Years later, a handsome prince came by, kissed her, and Chocolate Brown awakened.

The moral of this story is, you who read this article have been asleep, walking through the game of life in a stupor, not consciously aware of what you are doing. This speech represents the kiss of the handsome prince to wake you up.

Row, Row, Row Your Boat*

We are going to end this speech with a song. A round called Row, Row, Row Your Boat. You know the song. What I want you to do is to sing the song line by line. As you sing each line, we stop and I will make an interpretation of that line and then we will put it all together. So, let's begin.

The first line is,

Nolan: Row, Row, Row your boat. So let's sing it loud and strong with feeling.

Crowd: "Row, Row, Row your boat!"

Nolan: The song says, to row your boat, not someone else's boat or to let anyone row your boat. In other words, row your own boat and take care of your own business.

Now, the next line is, "Gently down the stream."

Crowd: "Gently down the stream!"

79

Nolan: It doesn't say up the stream, or across the stream. Too many times we go against the flow of life. And, we do, we create problems for ourselves. So, let's go with the flow of life.

Now, the next line is, "Merrily, merrily, merrily!"

Crowd: "Merrily, merrily, merrily!"

Nolan: It doesn't say, "Sadly, Sadly, Sadly," or "Depressed, Depressed, Depressed", "Angry, Angry, Angry!" Too much of our life in spent in misery. So, let us have a good time and enjoy ourselves.

Now, it's time to sing the whole song all the way through, so, let's hit it.

Again, let's sing it with power and feeling.

Crowd: Row, Row, Row your boat!

Gently down the stream!

Merrily, merrily, merrily!

Life is but a dream!

Nolan: In other words, when you row your own boat; your own boat and not anyone else's; then as you go with the flow of life, good things will happen. And, as you have a good time while you do it, life will become just as you want it not just a dream, your dream!

Thank you, very much!

*adapted from a presentation by Dr. Wayne Dyer

Whenever a warrior decides to do something, he must go all the way, but he must take responsibility for what he does. No matter what he does, he must know first why he is doing it, and then he must proceed with his actions without having doubts or remorse about them.

– Journey to Ixtlan, Carlos Castaneda.

Operating In Life

Philosophy in most cases looks good on paper. However, when it comes to practical or everyday situations, philosophy in many cases falls short. In other words, it is best to have a working or applied philosophical base to operate with any degree of confidence. Therefore, the next step in the "Synthesis of Thomas III" is to show how these concepts can be used in real life situations.

How I have operated in life is a function of at least four concepts, (1) The Milk Cow Syndrome (how we have become entrapped in a system that doesn't support us); (2) Feelings (a day-to-day system we can use to deal with life's issues and problems); (3) The Voice (How we can be guided from within); and (4) The Three R's (how we can effectively communicate with others). Some of these concepts I have discovered just recently (i.e., The Milk Cow Syndrome and The Voice) while the other two I have used for quite some time (Feelings and The Three R's).

Feelings Concept

I discovered the Feelings concept about twenty years ago while driving home one night after spending the evening at my favorite nightclub. As I drove home, I noticed tightness in my chest that was very uncomfortable. I had had this feeling many times before and it always bothered me. This night however, I decided to determine what the cause of the tightness was. So, I investigated this tightness by completely experiencing the feeling. I found to my surprise that the tightness went away and began to feel very good. The feeling was so good that I drove another 15 miles or so past the exit to my home. I pulled over to the parking area of a Texaco Service station and sat in the car for some time experiencing the great feeling and then I drove home. I processed the experience later and determined that the sensation I felt in my chest was an inner feeling around my heart. I related this sensation to past events and found that the feeling around my heart was an indication of trust.

This trust became apparent because I had it several times in the past, for example when

1. I drove my ten year old Karman Ghia from Minneapolis, MN to Norman, OK (Approximately 800 miles) with no brakes (my emergency brakes were rigged to stop the car) and I got home safely)

2. I drove the Karman Ghia from Minneapolis to Denver, CO with no starter.

3. I drove the Karman Ghia from Emporia, KS to Norman with no clutch. I shifted the gears by the sound of the engine.

4. My wife and I drove to the beach in Galveston, TX about 2:00 am one morning to see the stars. The tide started coming and as I tried to drive away the car got stuck in the sand. I was not worried one bit. We were rescued within fifteen minutes; someone with a Jeep came by and pulled us out.

5. I drove more than 150 miles on a very icy road between Austin and Dallas, TX. I knew as long as I could feel the road through tires I would be okay.

These situations are but a few of the experiences I've had where I knew I would be able to make it home or deal with the situation with little or no problems. It was the feeling around my heart that gave me the confidence.

In contrast to the feeling in my heart, I found when I had a feeling in my gut, I had better pay attention. The stronger the feeling I had in my stomach the more quickly I needed to respond. These two indicators, my heart and gut feelings have served me well since then.

The Three R's

My teenage children helped me to develop the Three R's. We had a confrontation two years after my divorce from their mother. Before the divorce, I had absolute power; after the divorce, I had zero power, and they knew it. The confrontation was over my giving them an order to do my bidding and they refused. It shocked me because they didn't back down. I lost for the first time in any kind of interaction with them and I didn't like it one bit. I realized that I had taught them to be independent of everybody but me.

I learned that connecting with them was more important than having them attached to me. So, I made a change. I started treating them as independent individuals and sought to understand them as much as I wanted them to understand me. It was also essential to realize that they were beginning to understand how to take care of themselves. As long as they were attached to me they couldn't learn from their own experiences. Fortunately, they broke the attachment. By doing so, it became possible for the three of us to go to the next level of relationships, by connecting with each other.

We never fought to the death again although we had many disagreements. I believe they understood that I would listen to them and treat them fairly. We have an excellent relationship to this day because they know I will listen to them and try to understand as much as I can.

The Milk Cow Syndrome

The Milk Cow Syndrome is an outgrowth of my experiences with my clients during the past seventeen years. I have had the experience of people draining me. When I first got into the metaphysical world, I learned that hugging was a good thing. However, there were some people that I hated to hug because I felt drained afterwards. It got so bad, that I would literally run from these people to keep from being drained. Since running away wasn't very practical, I decided one day to hug freely and as I did so, to my surprise and delight, I wasn't drained. I repeated this procedure several times to make sure that it worked.

The book, The Celestine Prophecy by James Redfield, presents nine insights to living a fulfilled life. These insights are really about establishing wholesome or connected relationships. Insight four to seven describes how we have learned to get energy from each other and the games we play to gain this energy. It further states that when we gain this energy we win and therefore feel good. However, when we are not successful we lose and therefore feel bad.

This description is an accurate representation of what happens in a system that is based on Win-Lose dynamics. In a Win-Lose system, the only way anyone can win is for someone else to lose. Since we haven't been taught how to tap into an unlimited energy source within each one of us, we must get energy from other people. Therefore, we have to set up people to lose even when they think they are winning. In order to guarantee this option we have created a process I call "The Milk Cow Syndrome." It allows each person to tap into other people at will depending on their ability to push the right button or squeeze the right udder.

The Voice

The Voice is again the result of an experience I've had while driving. I noticed that sometimes when I let go of having to be somewhere in a hurry and slow down, I could hear a voice inside my head. That is, a voice different and independent from the usual voice in my head that's usually referred to as an internal dialogue. Over the years, since then, I have learned to listen and trust that voice. This voice was especially helpful during my bout with prostate cancer this past year.

There is a problem with the voice; however, I am not able to access the voice at will. I either forget or get too wound up in life's experiences at the time to make the connection. So, I'm still working on the process.

All four of these concepts have helped me make much better decisions in my life. I am much more confident about dealing with any situation because I know I have help or guidance available to me. That is, when I am making "Conscious, Deliberate, Choices!" These concepts form one more set of tools that form the network in "The Synthesis of Thomas III."

The Milk Cow Syndrome

I absolutely do not believe in giving. If there is anything such as a sin, then the concept of giving is the epitome of sinning. I know you and I have been taught that giving is one of the best things we could ever do. However, look over the course of your life and determine how often when you gave, did you feel drained by the situation or other person? And, how often when you gave, did you receive back? Now, how can the feeling of being drained or not receiving be good? Besides, if you are giving all the time, how can you be in a position to receive, and then who can give to you? I have many clients and have observed many individuals who have trouble receiving. They almost refuse to have someone give to them.

So, what do you think about giving now? I'm not finished with this. I want to explain something called, "The Law of Life" on this planet. This law probably holds true all through the universe; however, I can't speak for the universe at this time. You know this law but you have never been taught anything about it at home, in school, religious institutions, work, or your community. What is the Law of Life?

I have not yet had anyone to initially quote the Law of Life. A law according to science is something that has no exceptions under the conditions it is stated, i.e., the law of gravity or law of conservation of matter and energy. You may break the law but you can't erase it. It's going to be there. So, again, what is the Law of Life?

I've heard many attempts to state the law, such as, "that everyone must die, survival of the fittest, you must breathe (close), and many others. I've asked this question in my workshops, classes, and during readings. After getting their answers, I get participants to come to an understanding of the Law of Life, by asking the following questions:

First Question:
    What do we breathe out specifically?

86

You might be surprised by the answers I get. The correct answer, of course, is carbon dioxide.

Second Question:
    What species on this planet thrive on carbon dioxide?

The correct answer is, "the plant kingdom – plants, trees, bushes, grasses, etc."

Third Question:
    What does the plant kingdom give off or breathe out?

The correct answer is "oxygen".

Fourth Question:
    What would happen if the trees got together and decided that because humans are destroying them at such a rapid and alarming rate, the trees would seek revenge and stop giving off oxygen?

And the answer is, of course, "We would die."

    What then would happen to the trees? "They would die, too."

So, "What is the Law of Life?" I usually get an answer, such as, reciprocate, or give and take. I state the law, simply as giving and receiving.

When I present the Three R's lecture (as seen later in this section), the last R is Redox. Redox is a term used in chemistry to represent the oxidation-reduction process. (Remember, my scientific background is based in chemistry. So, when I need metaphors about life processes, I rely on my chemistry background.) The Oxidation-Reduction process refers to an exchange of electrons. This exchange occurs in chemical reactions when elements and/or compounds exchange electrons to create more stable elements and/or compounds.

Redox, in the context of relationships, refers to an exchange or sharing process between individuals. So, you might ask what does all of this have to do with Milk Cows? Well, Milk Cows represent the process of giving; Milkers represent receivers. In the Civilized World or Matrix, there are givers or receivers. In other words, it's a win-lose proposition. The Matrix I choose to live in is based a win-win proposition; the process of giving and receiving.

We have been taught to give since we were born into the Civilized Matrix. Therefore, giving is natural. As a result, each one of us acts as a Milk Cow at one time or another. However, some individuals are more predisposed to be Milk Cows, and others are predisposed to be Milkers. An individual is not born a Milk Cow. They have to be programmed to become a Milk Cow by others within the Civilized Matrix, including their parents, siblings, friends, teachers, bosses, etc. These programs are installed, along with anchors that cause the individual to respond appropriately when the proper triggers are activated. The triggering device may be the look or sound of helplessness or a feeling of guilt, or it may be just a feeling the individual gets when they are around the Milkers. Triggering mechanisms are unlimited and insidious. Just when you think you have neutralized a trigger, there are more than likely, other triggers present that can be anchored to the same need to give up the milk.

So, in what ways do you act as Milk Cow? For instance, are you aware of the many triggering mechanisms present with you? Do you feel helpless around certain people, seemingly responding to them in ways you don't want to? Do you feel drained afterwards or emotionally letdowns, or even angry at the way you responded to the situation?

If you do, the real question to ask is, "Do you want to change, such that you are no longer drained in certain situations or events?" "Do you want to have relationships that are based on sharing?" "Do you want to be energized by life's experiences rather than the feeling of being letdown?" "Do you want to cease being a Milker?"

Now, once you have been committed to giving, it may be very difficult to practice "giving and receiving". In order to make this transformation, you will first have to understand that it is in your best interest to "give and receive". The problem is, people have written for years about giving and receiving without clarifying that it is different from the idea of giving.

Love in the Civilized Matrix, has even been equated with giving. My understanding of love is different. Love emanates from a connection with God, such that the expression God is love means to me that God is connected with everything and everything is connected with God. Therefore, in order to best express our connection with God is to not only maintain a conscious connection with God but also maintain a conscious connection with ourselves, as well as, with others and the rest of God's creation.

One of the best ways to establish a conscious connection with God and others is to connect with a conscious flow of energy. An exercise you can use to establish this connection is with what I will call the Connection Exercise. It is as follows:

Level I - Connection with Self:

1. You can start by closing your eyes and creating a second image of yourself and placing that image in front of you. Next, put yourself in the deepest relaxed state you can at this time. Don't worry about how deep it is or try to evaluate this relaxed state in any way. Any effort to do so will bring you out of this relaxed state.

2. Focus your attention on your heart and place this relaxed feeling in your heart. Let it spread throughout your body from your head to your feet and then one-foot in all directions around your body. Now bring this feeling back to your heart. You are now at level 0.

3. Now bring the energy feeling out the side of your heart, out of the side of your body, around and into the side of the image of yourself, through its heart and out the other side; then bring the energy around and into your other side and through your

heart again. Such that, the energy is how flowing in a circular channel through both hearts.

4. As you experience this circular flow of energy, notice how you feel and maintain the flow of energy. You are now connected with yourself and thus, practicing giving and receiving with yourself, loving yourself as it were. You are now at level 1.

Level II - Connection with God or Higher Self: I believe that since God or some higher power made us, then, there is a part of us that is God.

5. So, create in your mind an image of God inside of you, your God-Self. Close your eyes and repeat steps 3 and 4 of the above procedure. Once you have the flow of energy going between you and your God-Self, you have established a conscious connection with God, loving God as it were. This is level 2.

Level III – Connection with Others: Now, think of someone who drains you, preferably a lot. Don't make this choice difficult; just make the choice.

6. Close your eyes and create an image of this person and place the image in front of you. Again, repeat steps 3 and 4 of the above procedure. As you establish this flow, you are not concerned with the other person's energy; you are concerned only with the flow of your own energy. Let go of any influences you feel from them and you'll find it just as easy to establish the flow of energy. As the energy flows in a circular channel through both hearts, notice how you feel. Notice in particular how the energy feels as it comes back to you. If it doesn't feel good, you are still allowing their energy to influence you. As you let go of this influence, you'll find that after a while, you will start to feel much better. You will be reclaiming your own energy, empowering yourself and becoming whole

again with respect to that person. Maintain this flow of energy until you feel complete again. Under these conditions no one can drain you anymore. This is level 3.

Now, notice how the other person's image reacts to your circular flow of energy. Let their image react on its own free will without any expectations from you. As a result, you will get one of three reactions.

7. The person's image may act surprised and wonder, "What is this?" But then realize, "Oh, I like this!" Their image will then facilitate the connection by supporting the flow with their own energy. As the connection is made, notice that the circle of energy gets brighter and stronger.

8. The person's image may stand or sit there because it doesn't know what to do. So, you tell the person's image, "I want you to connect with me, by giving and receiving with me as I am with you, supporting the circular flow of energy with your own energy". Keep repeating this request until either the person connects or just remains there. If the person's image still doesn't support the flow of energy with his or her own, then say, "I want you to connect with me or go away". If the connection is established, OK; if not, let the person's image go away on its own. It's their choice. Whatever happens, either way, you'll be free of their ability to drain you and therefore be OK.

9. The person's image may go away on its own or it may try every trick in the book to trigger your need to give again. As you continue to keep the connection going, the person's image will realize you won't be giving anymore, so it will go away. At any rate, you will be free of that person's ability to trap you into a win-lose relationship.

91

When you understand the Milk Cow Syndrome, you will see how other people are able to rob you of your energy. You further see how you have been unconsciously playing a win-lose game whether you like it or not. If you enjoy living life this way, go ahead and enjoy it. If not, then use the Connection Exercise to eliminate all the relationships in your life that drain you of your energy. Then, convert each relationship into a win-win situation by establishing and maintaining a connection with each person. You will then have relationships that are much more harmonious. When that happens, you'll have a happier and more fulfilling life.

Another important point to notice in the art of giving and receiving with yourself first, is the idea of "Paying Yourself, First." It makes no difference whether it is with finances, energy, or relationships. When you pay yourself, first, you are (1) taking care of yourself; (2) empowering yourself, and (3) working toward wholeness. When you pay yourself, first, you have what you need and therefore have no need to control, exploit, or dominate others, and at the same time no one can control, exploit, or dominate you. As a result, you can play Win-Win with others.

In other words, you have a choice. As the Milk Cow or the Milkers, you live life more than likely as an automaton or robot. You may also feel trapped and under these conditions it may be hard to believe you have choices. If you want to change this situation, you must understand that you always have choices. The Connection Exercise can help you understand the many choices available to you at any time.

In order to employ the Connection Exercise, you must make a "Conscious, Deliberate, Choice" to live life differently. Once you consciously connect with yourself, God, and others, you will begin to live a life of CHOICES. Hell, to me, is a life where there are few, if any choices; and even those are bad. Heaven, to me, is a life with a myriad (beaucoup, a lot) of choices, and all of the choices are good ones.

Feelings: Learning To Use Your Feelings In Decision-Making Processes!!!

The word feelings can be defined in many ways, i.e., tactile (touch), sensation, or emotional. However, I would like to offer a different definition that will allow a more effective use of the word, according to the Synthesis of Thomas III. FEELINGS can be defined as an energy field you experience inside your body, preferably in the area of your heart or the stomach. This energy field is not to be confused with touch or emotional states. FEELINGS also represent a vehicle of communications between your outer, inner, and higher Selves. Your Outer self represents that part of you that experiences life's events. Your Inner self helps you to make sense, gain knowledge, and understanding from these experiences. Your Higher Self holds your overall life plan, the blueprint of lessons you are to have in this life. The Inner and Higher Self are constantly offering you guidance about your activities as you experience life. These messages are designed to help you deal with the complexities of life. You can always trust these FEELINGS. FEELINGS can't lie, although you may misinterpret them.

One way to access this vehicle of communications is to assume a power position. That is, sit the way you would sit when you feel very powerful and in control, such as, when you are the King or Queen of your own universe. This is your power position. You want to assume this position whenever you do "inner" work (work on yourself). Select an image from the past or create one that represents a safe place. Place yourself in that safe place. This safe place becomes your workshop. Now, focus on the energy in your heart and surround yourself with light. Let the energy from this light flow out of your heart and massage your entire body; and slowly change the light around you through the colors of the rainbow. The colors of the rainbow correspond to the seven energy points with your body, called chakras. See Figure 2 below. That is, see the light around you become RED, then ORANGE, then YELLOW, GREEN, BLUE, VIOLET, AND PURPLE respectively.

Now, think of someone you trust. Get an image of that person in your mind and feel the FEELINGS in both your heart and stomach. Now, determine if this energy is strongest in your heart or your stomach. If your FEELINGS are strongest in the area of your stomach or in between, then choose another person. You don't trust that person as much as you think. You want the strongest FEELINGS to be in the area of the heart. Your Heart Feelings let you know when you are in balance.

Figure 2
The Charkas

Charka	Placement	Color	Meaning
Crown	Top of head	Purple	Spirituality
Third Eye	Middle of Forehead	Violet	Intuition
Throat	Throat	Blue	Knowledge
Heart	Heart	Green	Healing
Solar Plexus	1 inch above navel	Yellow	Energy
Belly	Belly	Orange	Emotions
Root	Base of Spine	Red	Identity

Now, think of someone you don't trust. Get an image of that person in your mind and again, determine if this energy is strongest in your heart or stomach. So, are your FEELINGS strongest in your heart or stomach? If your FEELINGS are strongest in the area of the heart or in between, you trust that person more than you think. You want the strongest FEELINGS to be in the area of the stomach. These Feelings in the area of your stomach will let you know when you don't trust someone or are out of balance.

This exercise allows you to calibrate your FEELINGS, so, you can determine the differences between good or bad, yes or no, trust or alarm FEELINGS.

In any case, you can always trust these FEELINGS. You may want to use your mind to make decisions or tell you what to do, however, your mind is not equipped to know the truth no matter how hard it tries. It can only repeat the ideas and experiences you've collected from the past. It can deduce the truth in some cases but the results of this collection may not always be in your best interest.

Harmony And Balance

By observing the FEELINGS or energy in the area of your heart and stomach, you can monitor the degree of harmony and balance in your life. Most people try to monitor their thoughts to change or eliminate the negativity they create or are exposed to. If you are not successful or are having some difficulty using this method, then, the FEELINGS mode is for you.

As you go through your day, monitor your FEELINGS. If your FEELINGS are predominantly in your heart then you are balanced and doing okay. However, if your FEELINGS are predominantly in your stomach, then you are out of balance and are not doing okay. Remember sometimes you may have trouble determining where the energy is the strongest. When this happens, take time to relax (assume your power position, etc.)

Now, think of a problem, person, or event you have had difficulty resolving during the past week or two. Check your FEELINGS and determine where the dominant energy is, in your heart, stomach, or in between. If your FEELINGS are strongest in your heart, then the problem is okay, there is no need to worry, just chill out. If your FEELINGS are strongest in the area of your stomach, then something is wrong and needs to be resolved, you are out of balance. If your FEELINGS are strongest in your stomach, then, focus on that energy, concentrate letting your thoughts go free. An explanation will come to you that will describe what is wrong, out of balance or what you can do to resolve the situation.

When you get the answer, pay attention to your FEELINGS and determine if the energy is still in the area of your stomach. If it is, then ask again and repeat the process of setting your thoughts free, until you can obtain an answer you can deal with. When you can observe your FEELINGS or energy moving from your stomach to your heart (In other words, you are balanced again).

Goals

Getting what we want when we want it might be likened to having money in the bank. However, instead of money, it's energy! We not only need energy in the bank, we need to know how to access it as well. Energy in this case can be expressed or manifested in terms of our FEELINGS.

When goals are set, the difficulties encountered in reaching these goals can be placed in three categories: (1) Having the energy to create goals; (2) Clarity of goals, and (2) Sabotaging goals.

1) Having the energy to create goals is determined through meditation and your ability to maintain harmony and balance. Of course, you can maintain harmony and balance by monitoring your heart and stomach.

2) Clarity of goals is affected by an inability to know exactly what you want. This inability comes from not having a complete picture or understanding of what you want, as well as being too general or too specific.

3) Sabotaging goals arises because of conflicts between two or more goals or when a goal interferes with the beliefs or habits you use to deal with the experiences of life. Sabotage can also occur when negative energy is associated with a goal or through limitations you place on yourself.

Going For The Gold!

STEP I:

Assume your power position, go to your workshop; relax. Now, assume the attitude that you can get anything you want; where there are no problems, limitations, or barriers; nothing to stop you from getting what you want! If there were nothing to stop you, what would you be doing six months? One year? Five years, from now?

Now, think of a number between one (1) and seven (7). For the next (? – the number your chose) days do the above exercise. But this time write down your answer. Each time you write your answer, do not look what you wrote the previous day. On the (? + 1) compile your list from each day into one.

EXAMPLE:

Suppose you chose the number four (4). For the next four days, at the same time period, assume your power position, go to your workshop, relax and the "no limitations" reality. Write down what you are doing in six months, one year, and five years. Each day write your answer independently of the previous day's work.

On the fifth day, compile your answers and sort them according to their importance to your getting what you want. Then choose the top three, five or ten items.

STEP II:

Now that you are clear about what you want, just ASK FOR IT! The Bible says, "Ask and Ye shall receive!" Sit in your power position, and go to the deepest meditative state you can and "ASK FOR IT!"

STEP III:

After you have "asked for what you want", determine if the message was received, properly. Check the FEELINGS in your heart and stomach. If the FEELINGS are in your heart, it's yours! And you don't have to do anything! It will happen automatically! However, if the FEELINGS are in your stomach or in between, something is wrong. So, focus on your stomach (don't think, feel) and ask what is wrong? Or how you can change it? Or what do you need to do to get it the way you want it? Listen for the answer, and incorporate it in your compiled goal statement. Check your FEELINGS again, and repeat the cycle until your FEELINGS are entirely in your heart. It's now yours, LET YOUR INNER SELF GUIDE YOU; AND LET IT BE!!!

Meditation

Sit in your power position and go to your safe place. Focus on the energy in your heart and surround yourself with light. Let the energy from this light flow out of your heart and massage your entire body. Now, slowly change the light through the colors of the rainbow: RED, ORANGE, YELLOW, GREEN, BLUE, VIOLET, AND PURPLE. Now, think of a word you can associate with the way you feel, and begin saying that word quietly, over and over inside your mind. Remain in this relaxed state and keep saying this word for 24 minutes (one minute for each hour of the day).

Feelings And The "Inner" Voice

We all have voices in our head. These voices originate from a variety of sources. Remember when you've said, "That's my mother, father, or teacher talking? You see every significant authority figure that has tried to tell you what to do has a voice in your head. These voices are sometimes positive, sometimes negative, sometimes critical, and sometimes destructive depending on the circumstances. The voices are trying to help you, but may end up hurting you at any time. So, normally you can't trust a given voice since you don't know the source of that voice.

When you access your FEELINGS, it automatically shuts off all negative and external voices. The only voice that's left is your Higher Self; that voice you can always trust.

Forgiveness and Letting Go

Sit in your power position, go to your workshop; begin saying your word and relax. Close your eyes and bring an image of the person, yourself, or situation you are dealing with in front of your third eye (the middle of your forehead and between your eyes). With the image in front of you, ask if it is time to forgive yourself, the person, or situation, then, check your FEELINGS. If your FEELINGS are strongest in your heart area, you are ready to forgive. If not, then, "ask "What do I need to do to release this problem?" If an answer does not come then you need more time to process the problem; so, wait and resume the exercise at a later date. If an answer comes, deal with it until your FEELINGS move into the area of the heart.

When your FEELINGS are in the heart area, ask for the light of the Universe, God, Christ, or Buddha to appear over your shoulder. When the light appears, send the image of yourself, the person, or situation to the light and LET GO!

The Three R's

One of the most difficult skills a manager must develop is the ability to set aside his or her own perspective in order to understand the perspective of a fellow worker or manager. As managers, relating to workers and other managers is one of the more important things we do every day. However, we have difficulty at times with some workers or managers whose perspective is different or not recognizable to us. Managing, motivating, or communicating with this worker or manager is difficult at best. There is a way to overcome this problem. We can implement the Three R's Strategy.

The Three R strategies are especially effective in situations of conflict. It allows you a way of getting into another person's head to determine the how, why and what of their thinking process. In a situation involving conflict, we assume we know what the other person is thinking or that we know what they mean. In a normal situation, we may come very close to determining the nature of the other person's thinking and thereby, determine what they mean. In a situation of conflict, these assumptions can aggravate the conflict and cause added misunderstanding. In these situations, your emotions skew your ability to pick up information clearly, which inhibits your ability to determine what the other person is thinking or exactly what they mean. You might have a partial idea or even close but still are not there.

The Three R's strategies allow you to listen and get a feeling about the other person's position. Once you have an understanding of that position, then you have a chance to deal with that person. To use the Three R's strategies, you must first put aside your own position, pay attention, and then listen to the other person with an open mind.

The Three R's strategies are as follows:

1) **R1: Reality** - a function of your ability to see the other person's perspective and perception

a) Test your assumption to see where the worker is coming from

b) See the other person's view

c) The map is not the Territory

2) **R2: Rapport** - a function of your ability to build a bridge or connection with the other person

a) Cooperation not confrontation

b) Choose the Climate

c) Address the other party's needs

3) **R3: Redox** - a function of your ability to share or exchange

a) Create a deal where everybody wins

b) Dependent to Independent to Interdependent

c) Cooperation, Delegation, and Growth

R1 Strategy:

The R1 strategy revolves around the understanding that everyone has their own reality base that is unique to them. This base provides for a given person a basis for their perspective or "point of view" about the world around them (i.e., ideas, people, places, things or activities). The reality base also dictates that person's perception of the world (i.e., the looking glass that causes one to see things that are not there; ignore things that are; or distort things they don't agree with). Your perspective and perception are built on at least three factors:

1 The Heisenberg Uncertainty Principle - which states, simply, that you cannot know the location and speed of an object at the same time. If you know its location, you can't know its speed; and if you know its speed you can't know its location. This idea implies that where you are located with respect to an event or activities changes how you perceive it. Your perspective or perception changes with your state of mind.

2 Your ability to make use of your senses and emotions - You use your ability to see, hear, touch, taste and smell objects. Some people wear glasses, use hearing devices, and have trouble distinguishing between different contacts, tastes and smells. You may have trouble agreeing on what color an object is, how it sounds, what it feels like, how it tastes, or what it smells like, at one time or another.

How you feel emotionally also affects how you make observations, as you use your senses. The observations you make tend to reinforce your internal or emotional state or vice versa. Therefore, observations you make may be skewed by how you feel.

3 Your previous experiences - You have a vast database of experiences to serve as anchors that dictate how you catalog an event or activity. Traumatic or other significant experiences that you had in childhood and other times in your life forms anchors that force you to accommodate, delete, or distort data. Your perspective or perception, therefore, may be dependent on these previous experiences.

If you don't want to communicate or work with another person and at the same time you don't have to, then go on about your business and have a great day. However, if you want to communicate or work with another person, and/or you have to, then there are three things you must do.

1. You must accept that the other person's perspective or perception is right for them. It is not good or bad, right or wrong, it's just theirs.

2. You must seek to obtain an understanding about this perspective or perception. Remember, your viewpoint as well as theirs is only a map and not the

territory, itself. And what's more, you don't have to accept it as your own. However, you especially must seek to understand even if you know you won't agree with them.

3. You must show that person you have an understanding and can negotiate within it, as well,

With this understanding, you have built a bridge between you and the other person. The important thing about a bridge is that it goes both ways. We are always trying to get the other person to build that bridge to us. Apparently, the other person is trying to get us to build that bridge to them. So, either two bridges get built that don't meet or none at all.

So, when you build a bridge to the other person, they have that same bridge back to you. Now, just because you build the bridge, it doesn't mean that the other person will use that bridge. For instance, many people who tried to cross the bridge in the past were blown up just when they reached the middle of the bridge. Therefore, these people will have trouble crossing your bridge. It may take a week, a month, or 6 months to a year before the other person feels comfortable enough to cross the bridge. It may seem like a long time, however, do you want a year to pass and have the same communication problem? Or, would you want a year to pass and have the communication problem resolved? When you do, you now have a rapport built between you and the other person.

There is a disclaimer however; there are snakes out there. Snakes bite. That's how they survive, thrive, or protect themselves. Some people are like snakes and that means there's nothing you can do. You still want to connect with snake-like people because when you do, you are always one step ahead of them. In other words, you will be better able to protect yourself.

I truly believe that there very few real snakes, less than 1 per cent of the population. However, a lot of people, most of the ones we have a problem with, act like snakes to protect themselves. They seek to get you before you get them. These people, even though you must make the supreme effort, you can establish a rapport. And when you do, you can proceed now proceed to the R2 strategy.

R2 Strategy

Establishing the R2 strategy means that you must now pay attention and listen without judgment to the other person's point of view. (Remember, you don't have to like or agree with their point of view but you must allow them the privilege of having it). Give the other person feedback about your perceptions until you have a working understanding about their point of view. Most people (90 to 95 percent) will assist you in gaining this understanding. If they don't agree to disagree, let it go and do the best you can under the circumstances. Once you have a working understanding you can now build a <u>bridge</u> or <u>connection</u> with that person. The important thing about a bridge is that it goes both ways, so, when you build a bridge or connect with the other person; they have that same bridge back to you.

Most people want to establish a bridge, however, their anger or other emotional states may get in the way. This is a time for cooperation, not confrontation. When you establish a sincere interest in their situation and give them a chance to be heard, their emotions will more than likely dissipate. Choose the proper place and climate if at all possible. In order to establish the bridge or connection, make sure you let the other person know you understand their needs and will address them.

Now, once the other person's point of view has been heard you will now have a chance to provide your point of view. Your viewpoint can be best facilitated using "I-Messages".

"I messages" implies that you take responsibility for your statements or actions. Generally, people use "You Messages," which implies that they are blaming someone else for their problems.

ESTABLISHING CONNECTIONS BETWEEN
INDIVIDUALS

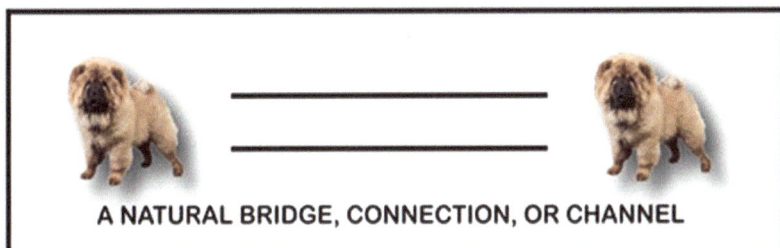

A NATURAL BRIDGE, CONNECTION, OR CHANNEL

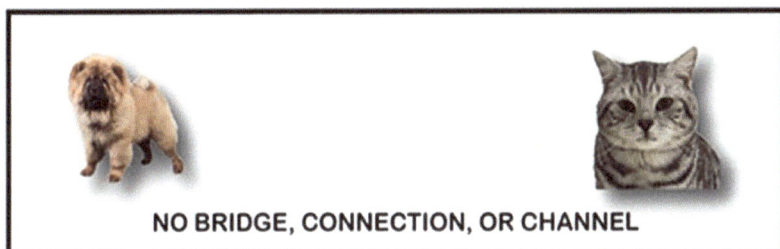

NO BRIDGE, CONNECTION, OR CHANNEL

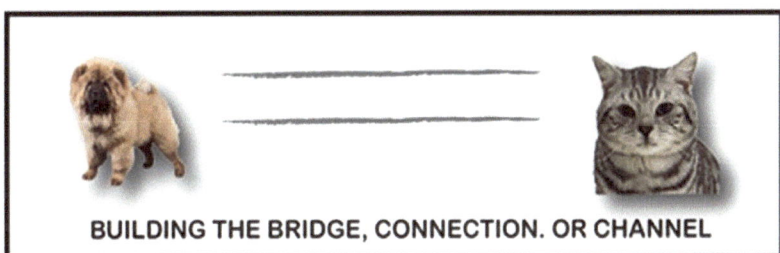

BUILDING THE BRIDGE, CONNECTION. OR CHANNEL

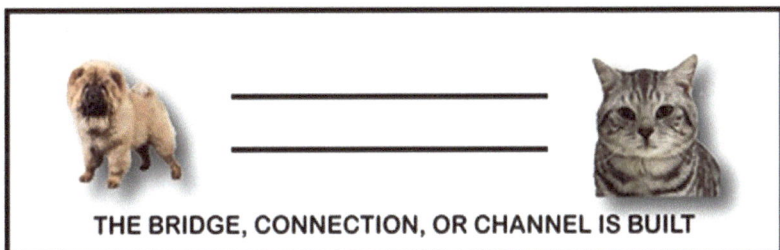

THE BRIDGE, CONNECTION, OR CHANNEL IS BUILT

Once you establish the bridge between you and the other person, the bridge or connection must be maintained. Maintenance of the bridge depends on your ability to pay attention to the flow of the interaction between you and the other person.

There is always the possibility that you will find someone in that 5 to 10 percent range who won't cooperate.

R3 Strategy

When you have established a working understanding of each other's points of view, you can now deal or negotiate with the other person. Negotiation should be thought of in terms of <u>sharing</u> or <u>exchanging</u> (i.e., to give and take). Sharing is a function of giving and taking something outside of you, while exchanging means to give and take something you both already have. Once you can establish this behavior, you can negotiate a "win-win" arrangement.

Establishing a win-win position means that you must understand what the other person really wants. You must consider that the other person does not want the same thing that you want, maybe something similar, but it will still be different. In most cases, what the other person wants is not something you even care about. Don't just make assumptions; validate them first. If you want the same thing, be creative in determining how the situation may be resolved.

If the person continues to be uncooperative, at the least you have information that will have deal with them in a better manner. And, you will probably be one step ahead of them which means you can make better decisions for yourself. In most cases, it is just a matter of time. It may take up to a year but do you want a year to pass and have the same problem or a potential solution.

It is your job as a manager to develop the people under you. You might consider that workers may be classified as dependent, independent, or interdependent. When workers are dependent (i.e., needs assistance in learning the job), use the "One Minute Manager" strategy to develop them into independence (i.e., can perform the job without assistance or direct supervision). Once a worker has reached an independent status, then, you can use "Team-Building" techniques to create an interdependent (part of an integrated whole) workforce.

Developing the people under you into a team means that you are willing to foster cooperation, by setting the standard for the group. One of the ways to increase cooperation is to delegate more responsibility to your worker. Remember, when you delegate, you must give the worker enough authority commensurate with the responsibility you assign to the worker. Delegation gives workers an opportunity to grow and therefore, fulfill their own needs for career development.

The Voice

The Voice is something we all have but may or may not be aware of, let alone listen to. The "Voice" can be defined as an inner source of wisdom we all have within us. It is available to help us, teach us, and guide us through life. If you believe in God, and that God made you, then you will understand that there is a part of you that is God. The "Voice", then, represents that part of you that is God. It is an independent part of you and therefore uncontrolled by you. More importantly, the "Voice" won't steer you wrong, lie to you, exploit you, or try to control you. It will however cause you to make decisions that may seem crazy or unintentional but decisions that turn out to be in your best interest.

There is ample precedence for the idea of an inner voice. One of the best explanations is found in Julian Jaynes' book, entitled, The Origin of Consciousness in the Breakdown of the Bicameral Mind. In this book, he speaks of ancient times before humans became civilized when they were governed by a divine voice. The gods talked directly to the individual through this divine voice. As long as these humans were isolated within their own areas, these inner voices worked very well. However, as migrations occurred due to wars, incursions, and natural catastrophes, this inner voice became less and less effective. Another and perhaps equally important event that weaken the efficacy of the inner voice was the invention of writing. Since the word of the gods could be written down and preserved, the individual became again less and less dependent on the inner voice. As civilizations flourished, most individuals began to ignore this inner voice and lost their dependence on this voice altogether. The exceptions were the priests and high priestesses that became the vehicles for the word of the gods.

The voice can also be described in terms of an inner consciousness that has connections with the best parts of an individual, the inner and higher selves. One of the difficulties of listening to the "Voice" is that there are other voices in our head. These voices originate from an external source. For instance, every person who has ever tried to teach, help, and control us has a voice in our head. Haven't you ever heard yourself saying? "That is my mother talking." "Those are my boss's words coming out of my mouth." Therefore, these external voices include your parents, siblings, relatives, ministers, supervisors, and teachers, among a few. As a result, most of us have multiple voices in our heads. There may be so many voices we may have difficulties in determining which voice to listen to.

The task we have at any time is to differentiate between the different voices within our heads. When the conscious mind is in control of our reality, all voices are active. However, external voices are only available when the conscious mind is in control. Therefore, when you relax and make a connection with your inner consciousness, the external voices become inactivated. This connection leaves only the "Voice" active.

"The Voice" has manifested itself to me in different forms. The first time it appeared, it caused the biggest fight I've ever had and perhaps the only real fight I've had.

> I was in the ninth grade at Paul Lawrence Dunbar High School in Little Rock, Arkansas. We didn't have an athletic field to practice or play on. The football and track events were held at Central High School's field, the infamous white high school that was integrated the year after I finished high school. Our practice field and gym classes were held at that time on a vacant lot behind a church approximately two blocks from the school.

> Sometime during the last of October or the first of November, I was participating in gym class. We were playing baseball. My side had made the third out and was headed for the field. The class "Bully" said, "I'm going to bat first next inning." It just so happened that it was to be my turn next. Before I could do anything, "A VOICE" came out of me and said, "YOU'RE A DAMN LIE!" Now I (Thomas) did not say that, I remember looking around to see who said that. I must say that it is still not my nature to curse in public. The Bully retorted

109

back, angrily, "What did you say?" And, again "THE VOICE" said again, "YOU'RE A DAMN LIE!" I was shocked, but I batted first anyway. When class was over, I rushed back to the gym because I knew he was going to beat me up, and frankly I was scared! I took a quick shower; went to pick up my books that were on the bleachers near the north side door, the one we entered when we come in from outdoor classes. As I was about to pick up my books, he entered through that door with an entourage of guys who were just itching to see him whip my "butt".

The Bully started talking, yelling about what he was going to do to me. (It occurs to me now that he had been upstaged and had to do something to show me that I couldn't just ignore his power). I remember him shaking his finger in my face and being scared as hell. I mean really scared to death. People like him were crazy and could really hurt you. I DO NOT LIKE PAIN!

I remember counting to ten! "At the count of ten, I put one hand at his neck and one between his legs, then I lifted him straight over my head in one swift motion (you know like weight lifters do. I think it's called a "clean jerk." I don't know how I knew how to do that). Then I threw him against the bleachers, pounced on him and began to choke him. The teachers, I think, came and pulled me off of him. I might have killed him. It all happened so quickly that it's hard to remember the sequence of events.

Now, I was really in trouble. I was being sent to the principal to be disciplined for fighting. I had never in my life been sent to the principal for disciplinary reasons. I was known as a "good" kid.

My books were thrown off the bleachers in front of the north central door. I began picking them up and the next thing I knew, the bully charged over and kicked me. I was kicked just below my left eye. Blood was everywhere. I was sent to my family doctor, Dr. O. B. White, who chastised me for fighting. (This was 1953). At least four or five stitches were required to close the wound. Dr. White told me that since I was fighting he would not anesthetize my eye. (It was probably nothing he could do anyway, I learned years later). So he sewed up the wound as I lay there. I don't remember any pain, I was probably still in shock and felt ashamed that I was fighting; yet I was extremely proud of what I had done.

The bully had kicked me when I wasn't looking. But I had beaten him. He was a coward. I now had a badge of honor. I surprised both him and myself and always thought I won the fight. Now I see that there was no winner. However, no one ever really challenged me after that incident.

After this experience, I understood that there are no winners in a fight. I beat you; you beat me; I lay in waiting for you and waylay you when you least expect it (or vice versa). It only ends with one or the other or both will become badly hurt or dead. This thought process was the beginning of my ability to run scenarios to determine possible endings. I saw possible endings to this problem, most of which I didn't like. I could get him back, he could in turn get me back, and it would keep on going until one or both of us would be dead.

I also was terrified of the enormous power and strength I displayed. I was so afraid that I put it away and vowed not to use it again. It was too awesome. So, I shut the power down and at the same time the "Voice", as well.

Although I thought I had shut the "Voice" down, it didn't shut down altogether. I believe it still took care of me and kept me on track from then on. The "Voice" appeared at the strangest times, usually when I was stressed from fear or when I knew I needed to do or say something and was afraid to. For instance, the "Voice" later manifested itself in graduate school, during Dr. Murphy's physical chemistry class. Dr. Murphy was head of the Chemistry Department at the University of Oklahoma. I was working toward a Master's Degree in Chemistry and taking Physical Chemistry. Dr. Murphy was the most feared instructor in the entire department and Physical Chemistry was one of the most difficult courses. This was also during early sixties when there were only four Black graduate students in the department. Once a week, Dr. Murphy would call on me. I was caught totally off-guard and had no idea what the answer was. I had studied; however, I was very afraid and would therefore go blank. In spite of this, an answer came out of me. It surprised me and I'm sure it surprised Dr. Murphy because he would call on me again and again. Each time the answer popped out, I had no idea where it came from and each time the answer was right.

I didn't associate my present time period with the voice from the fight in ninth grade or the voice in graduate school until I was telling someone in the late eighties about my proposal to my wife, Cecelia. I became divorced from my first wife, in the late seventies. For three years afterwards, I had a ball chasing women; it was a storybook time. However, as I approached my fortieth birthday, during the month of September, I realized that although I was having a ball chasing women, I didn't want to be chasing women at forty-five. Chasing women was a full-time job.

This period was also my wilderness years where I was beginning my initial metaphysical training. One of the main concepts I learned during this period was the concept of asking for what you want. It is written, "Ask and you shall be given." I believed in this saying, so I decided to put it to the test. I wrote on slip of paper all the attributes I wanted in a mate. I put in a request to my higher **self** for this person to appear and burned the paper. Two weeks later, someone appeared. She was exactly what I asked for, I mean exactly.

However, two months later, I gave her back. Although she was exactly what I had asked for I forgot about the things I didn't want. She had many of the most important attributes I didn't want in a female companion. So, I gave her back.

Within five days of letting her go, Cecelia, my wife of 30 years, let me know she was available. I had known her for about two years.

She was considered to be on the top of a couple of my friend's lists as the most attractive female at that time. However, she was unavailable to any of us. So, when I found out she was available I didn't waste any time and immediately asked for a date. Four months later, we were having coffee or a meal at a local cafeteria, when I spontaneously proposed. I swear I didn't do it. I was totally surprised. Cecelia said yes before I had time to think about retracting it. I didn't want to anyway.

I realized years later, it was the same voice that told the bully, "You're a Damned Lie," and the same voice that gave the correct answers to the questions from Dr. Murphy. The same voice I have since learned to rely on to help me deal with life's issues, solve problems, write speeches, lectures, etc.

The "Voice" again manifested itself a couple of years later at the end of my wilderness year's period. I was driving to the lake to go fishing. During my wilderness years, I went fishing three to five times a week. During these times, I would throw out my lines, so I didn't really catch fish unless the fish caught themselves. My real reason for going was to study or read. As a result, during this five-year period I read five to ten books a week. So, this time as I drove to the lake, I made my first conscious connection with the "Voice".

> I've found that when I drive and let go of day-to-day pressures, I'm able to enter into an altered state of consciousness. My conscious mind takes over the driving in a very safe way. As a result, I'm free to connect with my inner mind. I call connecting with my inner mind an altered state of consciousness.

As I drove to the lake, I realized that I was holding a conversation with something other than the conscious me. In other words, there was another voice in my head. Now, once I have an experience such as this, I seek to recreate it. I was successful and since that time have had many dialogues. When I want to create something, like a workshop, lecture, or speech, there are times especially while driving I have been able to access this voice. For instance, I spontaneously created the first draft of the

Dunbar Reunion speech while driving on I-25 north between Trinidad and Pueblo, Colorado. When I have questions I can't answer or issues I'm dealing with, and I am able to access the "Voice", I get the answers I need.

Sometimes, I may go for long periods of time without making contact with the "Voice." Recently, as I was driving to Dallas, the "Voice" appeared. It had been a long time since I had been in contact with the voice. So, like an old friend I asked, "Where have you been?" The reply was, "It's not where we've been, it's where you have been!" My challenge then is to maintain contact on a regular basis. When I do, "Life is Good!"

Book Two

Every time a man sets himself to learn, he has to labor as hard as anyone can, and the limits of his learning are determined by his own nature. Therefore, there is no point in talking about knowledge. Fear of knowledge is natural; all of us experience it, and there is nothing we can do about it. But no matter how frightening learning is, it is more terrible to think of a man without knowledge.

– The Teachings of Don Juan, Carlos Castaneda

Who Am I?

The next step in understanding the "Synthesis of Thomas III" is to understand some of the more important events that have shaped my life. This section then becomes an autobiographical sketch in three parts, each giving a different description of how I became Thomas III. First, there is a description of what I learned from my parents. Each parent gave me a different reference to guide me. My mother taught me to be myself, while my father taught me to persevere. These references form the foundation of what I have come to be.

Second, there is a description of my evolutionary development into Thomas III. It occurred over three periods of my life. Each period describes different versions of Thomas: "Determine", The Doubting Thomas, and Thomas III. These three periods were not discrete, as two periods overlapped at any given time. "Determine" was my nickname in high school. It characterized a period of time when I relentlessly, forged trails toward goals that I deemed most important to me. At the same time, the seeds of the Doubting Thomas were also sown, as there were certain events where I just was not able to overcome. Thomas III represents the final stage of my development that is, at the same time, a continuing process.

Third, Thomas is one person with many faces. Each face represents a different part of Thomas III depending on my orientation to internal or external goals. The Faces of Thomas also represent the different parts of me I must integrate to become a whole person. One of my favorite philosophers, Gurdjieff indicates that this is the goal of the mastership. He reports that we have many "I's" to represent the different faces we use to interact with our internal and external environments. He further reports that we must integrate these "I's" into one.

Thomas is the name of choice for me. People who don't know me, especially whites want to call me Tom. I don't like the name Tom, although I do allow my family and perhaps a few others to use the name. I consider the name "Tom" to be degrading and endearing at the same time. Only a few people have the permission to use that name with me.

This unique perspective has been a source of difficulty for me during each period of my life. I've rarely felt connected with the people around me. I've felt like an outsider and have had this feeling since childhood. I've felt like I didn't belong because I felt smarter than most of those around me; or because I wasn't the best at what I did; or the fastest runner on the track team; or I couldn't triple tongue on the French Horn; or was the only Black person at most of the early jobs I had.

Thus, in the Synthesis of Thomas III, knowing who I am, where I came from, and where I intend to be, gives me knowledge of myself that I need to become and be a whole person. It further describes the evolutionary process of becoming Thomas III; as well as helps me identify the defective patterns of behavior and thus find ways to resolve them.

Motto:
Just Be Thomas and Then Persevere
The Ugly Duckling

My mother always told me to "just be Thomas" and my father taught me the value of perseverance. It took me many years to understand what they meant and even more to apply it in real life. For years, I see now that I didn't like myself. First, I didn't want people to know what I was really like because I didn't think they would like me. Second, I didn't seem to be like everyone else. I seemed different than most of the people around me. In fact, only one person in high school seemed to be even remotely like me. And third, I didn't seem to have natural abilities in sports or music, although I did participate in track, band, and choir. At the same time, the only thing I seemed to be the best at — academics — didn't seem to have the same value, especially with the girls.

I had no identity of my own because I didn't know who I was, or for that matter, who I could be. So I tried to create a persona that everyone would like and so attempted to become super cool and aloof. I was the proverbial "Ugly Duckling." It seemed that all around me people were able to make good social decisions. Although I was able to make good decisions academically, it didn't matter because I really wanted to be popular socially. My being good academically only mattered to other students it seemed when they wanted answers to my test questions.

My need to be popular was so strong that I made a very stupid decision. I decided not to try to become valedictorian (I knew I could if I wanted to). Many students have made this same decision for similar reasons I'm sure. Smart people didn't seem to get recognition. I want you to understand, this is the dialogue that was going on inside my head. Whether or not my fellow students actually felt this way is greatly in question and probably not true.

At the end of many speeches and workshops (including the Dunbar Reunion Keynote Speech), I use the Ugly Duckling story as one of my three closing statements. My conclusion from the story is:

"If you are a swan who's trying to be a duck, you are all messed up!"

"If you are a duck trying to be a swan, you are messed up as well!"

However, I didn't understand the continuing advice from my mother, "Just be Thomas!" I just wanted to hear those blessed words from the cheerleaders,

"Thomas, Thomas, He's our man, if he couldn't do it nobody can."

That view of life was crazy I know now. My natural abilities came in academics; however, I put my best efforts in playing the Mellophone horn, (an e-flat instrument that was used to replace the French horn in marching bands or concert bands if they couldn't afford French horns), singing in the choir, and participating in football and track. I didn't have natural abilities in any of these areas; however, I was able to excel in track and do fairly well in of these areas and later on with the French horn.

I know now that although natural abilities can help you to be good at what you do, there are strategies for developing skills you can become really good at what you do. Therefore, we can become good performers with proper training, practice and discipline. Training with proper instruction is paramount to good skill development because you need to know the "what, how and why" of these techniques as well. Practice is next because repetition helps you to learn these skills so that you can perform them without thinking about what you have to do. Discipline is needed to help you maintain the practice schedule, perform the repetitions in the proper way and keep your mind focused at the same time.

It took me years to understand the value of good training. My father taught me the value of perseverance through my participation in scouting. I became an Eagle Scout at just about the earliest age possible. However, it wasn't until years later that

I was able to apply the idea of perseverance to training, practice and discipline on my own.

I've been developing a training plan for myself over the past 20 years. I believe I finally have obtained most of the elements necessary to complete this plan. This plan contains several components, including spiritual, psycho-emotional and health.

The spiritual component creates the foundation that allows me to deal with any situation that occurs in my life. How you deal with any situation depends on the perspective and perception you have at that time. Does the situation offer you an opportunity? Is it a distraction or does it overwhelm you? Whether you see it as an opportunity or distraction depends on your sense of balance at that time. A sense of balance means that you have taken a neutral stance in life, taking neither a positive or negative perspective (See the explanation of "The Tree" at the end of this article). A neutral stance allows you to make the best possible decisions in any situation without being encumbered by your emotions. Emotions, whether positive or negative, can cause you to lose your contact with your inner selves and thus put you at risk of making decisions that are not in your best interest. Emotions can be used to identify the state of being you are in as long as you don't lose perspectives.

The spiritual component helps you to establish and/or maintain this neutral stance through a sense of connectedness to yourself, others, and God. Thus, when you are connected, you are able to interact with your environment in a balanced way under any condition, any place and any time. In this way, you are able to maximize your ability to learn and get the most out of any encounter.

The psycho-emotional plan helps you to maintain a balanced state of mind by reducing or eliminating the effects of unconscious reactions that limit your ability to deal with a given event. Most of us have been programmed to respond to a given event in ways that do not serve us. The psycho-emotional plan helps us to identify the anchors that trigger these programs, then neutralize or eliminate them. There is something called emotional fitness.

> Emotional fitness can be compared to a stream of water. When there is no water there, the stream is very easy to cross. Therefore, you are free and clear to make choices. (Hell can be described as a state of few choices that are all bad. Heaven can be described as a state of many choices that are all good.) Each day you try to cross the stream it gets higher and higher. When the stream is around your ankles, it's still easy to cross — your feet just get wet. When the stream is around your knees, it's still fairly easy to cross. If you fall down you just get wet. Now, when the stream reaches your waist, you are now in trouble, because if you fall down you can be swept downstream and are in serious harm. When the stream reaches your neck, you're now in serious trouble, immobilized. You don't want the stream to reach above your knees because you only need one more event to put you in serious trouble.

The psycho-emotional plan offers you a way of maintaining the water below your knees. When you can operate under these conditions, life is good.

The health plan helps you to deal with the issues that are caused by breakdowns in your spiritual or psycho-emotional conditions. The body is an amazing autopoietic system, that is, it has the ability to continuously renew itself and regulate this process in such a way that the integrity of its structure is maintained. When the body is maintained under optimum conditions, it is able to protect itself. Spiritual or psycho-emotional breakdowns seriously affect the body's ability to respond to a given threat or its ability to deal with chronic or acute conditions that are already in place.

When these three individual plans, training, psycho-emotional, and health are utilized in concert with each other, then I feel free to set and achieve my day-to-day or long-term goals. And, as I operate in this fashion, I am no longer an ugly duckling.

The Tree

"The Tree" represents a system of thought that challenges the concept of the "Power of Positive Thinking" process. Thousands, if not millions of people have used positive thinking for some time. However, I believe this process has several drawbacks. As a result, I would like to introduce another process that will address these problems.

The Tree[1]

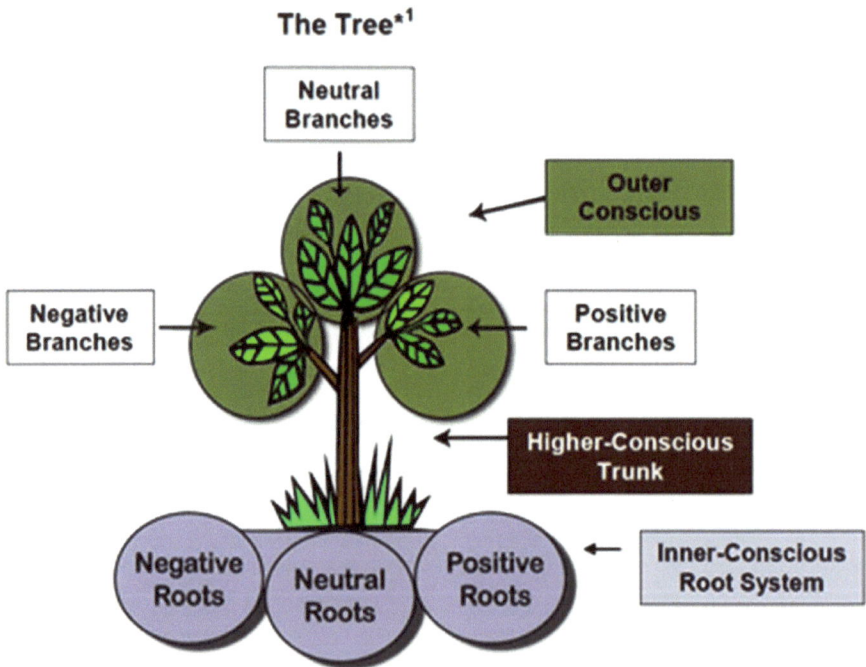

*[1]"The Tree", developed by Thomas J. Nolan, III and Susan Jennings, 1987

I understand what the "positive thinking" process attempts to accomplish. Its objective is to eliminate the powerful negative thought patterns or those thought patterns that create limitations or barriers that prevent us from accomplishing our goals. These thought patterns could cause emotional problems or even illness. It is hard to stop these thought patterns and it seems the more you try to eliminate them, the more powerful they become. What can you or I do to reduce, if not eliminate, the effects of these thought patterns?

My solution to the problem of reducing or eliminating the power of negative thought patterns is "The Tree," which can be explained as follows:

> "The Tree" is a metaphor for how we deal with situations we find ourselves in. It is composed of three component parts: 1) the trunk, 2) the root system and 3) the branch system.
>
> 1. The Trunk – represents the higher-conscious mind, that part of our mind that contains our blueprint for the lessons we will have in this life. It also is the seat of our connection with God or "All That Is."
>
> 2. The Root System – represents the inner-conscious mind; that part of our mind that contains our programmed thought patterns. It is also the seat of our inner consciousness that contains the knowledge and understandings we have gained during this lifetime.
>
> 3. The Branch System – represents the outer-conscious mind; that part of our mind that perceives and interacts with the events of our life. It is also the seat of our outer consciousness that deals with the outside world.

As we deal with people and/or events in life, we must make decisions about how we interact with these people or events. How we interact depends on the perceptions and perspectives we choose at that time. The choices we make then depend on how we access information from our inner-conscious. The perceptions or perspectives we exhibit at any time depend on what part of the subconscious mind we access.

The Root and Branch Systems each can also be described in terms of three sub-component parts; a) negative, b) positive and c) neutral.

1. Negative – represents the approach to life that leads to difficult, harmful or bad experiences.

2. Positive – represents the approach to life that leads to happy, healthy or beneficial experiences.

3. Neutral – represents an approach to life that allows you to live in the present and neutralize the roller coaster effect derived from going back and forth between good and bad experiences.

When we make a decision to act in a given way, that decision is influenced by the attitude we have at the time. The attitude we have is dictated by that part of the subconscious we are accessing. When we feel good we are accessing positive roots or when we are feeling bad we are accessing negative roots, i.e., imagine a line going from the branch in the positive side of the tree all the down to the positive root system.

Let's assume that you are having an experience, and as a result, something causes you to access the negative root system (imagine a line from the negative side of the tree going all the down to the negative root system). Once you have accessed the negative root system, your outlook is going to be negative. As time goes by as long as you are accessing the negative root system, your outlook will become increasingly negative. Remember some experience you've had in the past where you felt just this way. How did you feel? At this stage, never say things can't get worse because it will. I've experienced this condition many times in my life.

I felt controlled by this negative frame of reference and over the years searched for something I could use to change this condition. There were periods when I felt very good and there were those periods, sometimes over a six-week period, where I felt trapped by negative experiences. I tried positive thinking techniques; however, the negative frame of reference always came back. I call this process of going back and forth between the negative and positive sides of the tree the Roller Coaster Effect. The problem is you can't have a positive effect without a negative effect; once you set up a positive condition you automatically set the negative condition. Once you are on the Roller Coaster, your choices are very limited.

During the late 1970s, I learned relaxation and meditation techniques. I found that by using relaxation or meditation techniques I was able to move my consciousness to the trunk of the tree. Within the trunk of the tree, you have choices. Now I was able to choose the Positive Side of the tree whenever I wanted to. I chose the positive frame of reference, but I was still heavily influenced by the Negative Side of the tree.

Many disciplines speak of living in the moment or in the here and now. Other disciplines speak of limiting emotional involvement while others say that life is an illusion so let go of the illusion that entraps you. The Samurai Warrior goes even further by suggesting that we "Expect Nothing; Be Prepared for Anything." All of these disciplines suggest to me a neutral involvement with life. I know that most of you will think that "neutral" means that you are totally out of it. However, it is my view that you can be totally involved without being controlled by external circumstances. To achieve this state of mind, you can abide by the following guidelines:

The Neutral Frame of Reference Guidelines
- No judgment
- No blame
- No guilt
- No shame

Implementing the Neutral Frame of Reference strategy can be best described by the Umpire Story.

The umpires after one baseball season were very upset because of the way the players were responding to how the umpires called balls and strikes. The umpires had a convention and invited their three best umpires to act as consultants to show the best way to determine the calling of balls and strikes.

The first umpire got up to make his presentation and said, "Why are we here? It's so simple; all you have to know is call a pitch when it passes over the letters a ball; and when the pitch passes over the knees a strike!"

The second umpire got up and said, "Aw, please! He doesn't know what he's talking about. When the pitch passes below the knees, it's a ball; and when it passes below the letters, it's a strike."

The third umpire got up said, "Forget everything you've heard because it doesn't make any difference at all. A ball is a ball and a strike is a strike but it ain't nothing until I call it!

You can see then that whatever perspective you choose is not dependent on anything but your own choice of perspectives. In other words, you must decide to make a conscious – deliberate – choice about the way you deal in any situation. I didn't say it was easy. The difference is whether or not you are able to achieve and maintain a balanced state of mind. As described in previous articles, one of the best ways to achieve and maintain this state of mind is through the circular flow of energy exercise described in the article, "The Milk Cows Syndrome." Again, as you are able to maintain this state of mind, "life is good!"

The Three Modes of Thomas:
Determine, The Doubting Thomas, and Thomas III

The next step in understanding "Who I Am" in relationship to the Synthesis of Thomas III is to look at the events that led to the evolution of Thomas III. Occasionally, we experience events that are defining moments. That is, an event becomes associated with you or you with the event for the rest of your life. As I have learned to "just be Thomas" I have had many defining moments that have helped me to evolve into the person I want to be. I have had three significant defining moments that helped me create my persona for that period of my life. One moment was when I became Determine, the second when I became the Doubting Thomas and the third when I became Thomas III.

Determine
My persona, Determine appeared during my efforts to make the track team in high school. I first went out for basketball, remembering how the girls swooned over those dudes from Langston High School of Hot Springs, Arkansas. I wanted to be popular with the girls so I went out for basketball. I had no idea how to play the game of basketball and certainly didn't have natural talent. In those days you needed natural talents because the coaches didn't have time to spend with every player. There just weren't enough coaches to give you that special attention. Since I didn't know what to do and I hadn't played basketball before, I had no sense of where I was supposed to be at any given time on the court. I could dribble at little bit, but I couldn't shoot. Needless to say I didn't make the first cut.

I wanted to play football and later made the team although I wasn't very good at football, either. I was a hard worker. I won most of the running drills; I may have been the fastest man on the field in football clothes. However, I hated tackling or hitting other people and I certainly didn't like anyone tackling or hitting me. I tried catching; however, Rusty (our quarterback) threw the ball so hard it hurt catching it. I made the team and played third string halfback. I traveled with the team and the best play I ever made was a tackle on a punt return. I was the first one down the field. At least, I think I did the right thing. No one chewed me out, but no one congratulated me either. Anyway, I felt good about it.

I also tried baseball and made the team because I had the money to pay the American Legion ball fees. I played right or left field where I would cause the least damage. I was a liability to the team. I couldn't hit very well, if at all. I was born left-handed and was trained to use my right hand to protect me from being beaten in school like my dad was. (They did that in those days). I batted cross-handed and struck out a lot. I couldn't catch fly balls, especially at night; I would lose the ball in the lights. Ground balls were just as bad; they went right between my legs. My best performance came in the last game I played when I got a walk. The players commented after the game, "And Nolan got a walk, Wow! Again, there was no one to coach me on the proper techniques of catching or hitting and I couldn't learn on my own. I did learn the proper way to hit and catch in my late twenties when my brother-in-law showed me how.

You get the picture by now. I was not a very good athlete. Not in basketball, football or baseball. I had similar results in boxing, although I won the match because the other guy got disqualified because of low blows. He would fake hitting me in the head and as I moved my hands to protect myself he would hit me in the stomach. I hit him a lot so I wasn't very bad. I just didn't know what I was doing.

Since all of these efforts didn't work out, I went out for track in the tenth grade and found a home. The defining moment of this period came as I tried to make the team. First of all, we didn't have a track to practice on or host meets. This was the case for most Black schools in Arkansas as this was the period of "separate but equal" arrangements. We had to use Central High's stadium for football games and track events. We held football practice in a makeshift field behind the school and played home games at Central High's Stadium. There were even worse conditions at the first high school I attended. Dunbar Junior and Senior High Schools didn't even have a practice field. Vacant lots were used as practice fields. When integration became a distinct possibility, the Little Rock Public School system built a new high school and named it Horace Mann. That way, white kids would not have to go to a school named after a black person if they were forced to go to a black high school.

For track practice we were able to use Central High's track. However, we had to wait until they finished practice, then we shared the track with Philander Smith College (a local Black college) track team. The incident that created the first defining moment came when we were still at Dunbar. Our practice field was about three blocks from the school at the Dunbar Community Center. The center was located on a square block area. For several weeks before track season started, we practiced there.

Our miler who was very good and probably a champion miler in Arkansas, was running a practice mile. One of the guys was pacing him, playing the role of the rabbit. After two laps, he couldn't keep up, so I asked our coach if I could be the rabbit for the rest of the way. My father was there, although I didn't remember him being there. Years later in my early forties, he told me this same story. I had confronted him for not being at my sporting events. He told me that whenever he was around anything that I was involved in, I would almost break my neck trying to please him. Anyway, I was determined that the miler was not going to catch me and lap me. I went all out. He did not catch me. However, I passed out at the tape.

The next incidents occurred shortly afterward during the trials to see who would make the team. I participated in two trials, the 220- and 440-yard dashes. The English measurement system was used in those days. I don't remember trying to qualify for the 100-yard dash because I was too slow coming out of the blocks. Everyone beat me out the hole. I may have qualified third. The 220-yard dash was a different story. Again, I was left in the hole; however, as the race went on, I passed each runner, one by one and caught the last one at the tape. The last race was the 440-yard run. Again, I was left in the hole, and again, I passed each runner one by one and caught the last one at the tape.

Well, someone said, that dude can really run! He's really determined! Another person remembered my efforts at being the rabbit for our miler in the mile earlier and said, "Yeah, he is really determined, let's call him that." My nickname became Determine. It was one of the proudest moments of my life.

The Doubting Thomas
The Doubting Thomas syndrome occurred over many years. It was installed very slowly and has many anchors that can be activated to bring out that part of me. I will list several ways these anchors were installed or reinforced. They include girls, athletics, music, dancing, mostly things where I didn't consider myself to be the best or at least very good.

High School
In high school I considered myself to be a wallflower. I wasn't popular with the girls. I was afraid. Popularity was probably what I wanted most, to be respected, and to be well thought of. I didn't feel a part of any group. I knew I was smart, and that seemed to work against me. I didn't seem to have the skills that other kids valued, i.e., great athletic prowess, great singing voice, smooth talker, or coolness of being the dude. I did run track, but I wasn't the "Main Man"; I did sing, but I didn't have the lead voice; I taught myself how to fast dance but I wasn't the one everyone talked about. The one thing I was good in — academic achievement — didn't seem to go over with the girls.

High School Girls
It seems that the bottom line for me was my strong need to be accepted by females. It isn't ironic that one of my homeboys in college wrote in my yearbook my senior year, "Don't let the girls get you down." I didn't even realize he knew me that well.

One of the greatest defining moments for the Doubting Thomas syndrome occurred at a youth camp. I was a lifeguard and had an opportunity to have sex with one of the girls. I had no idea what I was doing and twice failed miserably. It was one of the most embarrassing moments of my life because some of the other guys knew about it, too.

I carried this shame for years. As I processed this event again in my fifties, I realized that my not knowing what to do was probably the best thing that could have happened. If I had been successful, it would have been my luck for the girl to get pregnant and where would that have left both of us? I now see that it could have been the best thing that could have happened.

Nearly 20 years ago, I met this same girl, now a good-looking, successful lady. She was present at what could be called one of the crowning achievements of my life. All of a sudden, my highest point became my lowest point. She told a friend of hers that I was a former boyfriend. I panicked. I didn't know what to do or how to act. I believe she thought I was high-siding her (being aloof). I wanted to talk to her but still didn't know what to do. I know now that she didn't even remember that past event. A couple of years later, I had a chance to talk with her. I explained to her my memories about that past event and how it had affected me all these years. When she finally remembered, she smiled. At this time, I was at a point in my life where I was secure enough about my manhood and had no need to prove to her that I knew what to do. I had killed a ghost. What's equally important is that the girl I selected grew into a beautiful, vibrant and successful lady. At least I had good taste.

High School Track

I wasn't a good athlete, except for track, and of course I felt track was the exception, not the rule. I was also good in academics, and again I dismissed that as being an exception. What I really wanted was to be popular. Even though I made the track team, I wasn't the best runner. I was the third fastest man on the team three years in high school and four years in college. Since I wasn't the fastest I didn't feel like I was very good. I wanted to be the best and third was not good enough.

High School Music

This same attitude played itself out in music. I played French horn and sang in the choir. I started in music with the band in the seventh grade playing Alto horn and the Mellophone. In my ninth grade year at Dunbar, we got two French horns. I really wanted

133

to play one; and they were so beautiful. However, the band director gave one to a baritone horn player and the other to my best friend who played the trumpet. I told my Dad and he told me to go to the band director (the same one who caught me smoking) and ask why he didn't choose me. He especially told me not say my Dad told me to ask him, but I did anyway. I said to him, my dad wants to know why I am not playing French horn. His reply was, "You tell your dad to call me and I'll tell him why!" And that was the end of that.

Now, during this time, most of the music for the horns was in the key of F. The Mellophone and Alto horn are in the key of e-flat. I had to learn to transpose most of my musical parts on the fly by playing one whole note down, which I was able to do very well. That didn't seem to be a big thing to me. I tried to get one of the French horns the next year. By then the band director had moved on and the former baritone player had graduated, as well. I tried to force the issue with the next band director, but someone had been training to play the French horn in beginner's band. Since I thought I had seniority, I took the horn, but was forced to give it up by the new band director. I was finally able to play a French horn when we moved to the new high school, Horace Mann. The school bought a complete set of new instruments for the transformed Dunbar Junior High School.

I went to college on a track and band scholarship. I was given the leadership role for the French section because the current section leader got drafted. I remained section leader for three and a half years. I wasn't the best in technique because I played third horn all through high school and for one semester in college. Therefore, I never developed the triple tonguing techniques. However, I did have a soulful sound and I believe very few people could make the horn sing the way I could.

Throughout all this time, there was an underlying fear based on the things I couldn't do well. It was now installed and growing. There are parallels to this story, with my ability to dance and sing. In all of these activities, I wanted to be the best: the fastest runner, the lead singer and the best dancer. It seems that in all of these activities, I was close to the top, usually about the third in line. I wonder if it has anything to do with being the third generation Thomas, destined to be the third best throughout his life.

I now recall the poem, "Be the Best of Whatever You Are!" by Douglas Molloch. I've heard this poem many times over my lifetime. I guess I've been in denial because I never really applied the theme of this poem to myself. It has very much the same theme as the words, "Just be Thomas" from my mother. Sometimes, it almost takes a lifetime for an idea to make sense. I am including this poem at the end of this article.

College

I went to a college out of state to get away from my own image of myself and thus, create a new me. However, since I didn't realize how this image of me was installed in the first place; it was more of the same. I didn't erase the old anchors, I just reinforced them. In track, for instance, I was the third best runner all four years I was there. I ran third leg on all the relays. I was chosen one of three captains my senior year. There were three seniors and all three were captains, so I assumed that it was because I was a senior and not because I was good.

We had a very good track team, winning two conference meets. Because we had very good relay teams, we entered the NAIA national meet in Sioux Falls, SD in 1961. I saw Bob Haynes, Ralph Boston, and Wilma Rudolph. Bob Hayes won the 100 yard dash; I believe it was his first major win. Tennessee State placed second in the meet because he won four events and placed second in another. Our Mile Relay team placed second in the Mile Relay. We ran second to Texas Southern. I got a silver medal and found out ten years later, that we were All-Americans. So, I'm an All-American

I was French horn section leader, three and half years in band. I was in constant fear that the band director would select someone because they were better technicians than me. They weren't that much better and I see now that overall, including sound I was among the best.

135

Again, behind all of this was fear. And, the biggest fear of all was my fear of females. One of the reasons I believe I had such a good sound playing the French horn was my sensitivity, something I haven't written about to this point. I've always been sensitive, having the ability to cry at any time, or more importantly, an ability to empathize with people, to feel their pain as it were. It took me until my fifties to realize that most of the time the emotions I felt around other people didn't come from me — it came from them. If I feel fear and the other person feels fear as well, both fears together may seem off the scale.

Because of this fear, I couldn't let people get too close to me, so I became aloof, trying to create a super cool image so no one would know how I felt. Needless to say, instead of drawing females to me I pushed them away. Another tactic was to select someone who either wanted someone else or at least wasn't available to me. Or better still, I reasoned that I couldn't deal with them because my anxiety was just too great.

When I did attempt to talk with someone, I didn't have a conversation, (a rap) so I talked about current events, life or ideas I had. My attempts at "raps" were usually too sensitive, abstract, or something that seemed to me to be something the girl thought was lame. I just didn't know how or what to talk about. I will write more about this later.

Graduate School

I have already written about this experience earlier when I described the events of Dr. Murphy's physical chemistry class. Dr. Murphy was very intimidating and for the first time I was taking a course that seemed difficult to learn. His reputation preceded him, as he was head of the physical chemistry department and was described by most students as being a very difficult and feared instructor. I was also having difficulty staying up with the class materials. I studied with a group of people and that helped; however, as I see now, the materials weren't difficult to learn, my fear just got in the way.

I had another experience where I really got in over my head. I had dreams of a double major in math and chemistry on the master's level. I enrolled in an advanced differential equations course. Within a week, I realized that I didn't belong there. My ego, however, wouldn't let me drop the course right away. Upon investigating other options, I found that I had enrolled in the advanced section of the advanced differential equations course. Somehow, I enrolled in the wrong section. I switched classes and immediately knew I was okay.

Work – Research Engineer

My first job was with the North American Aviation Company, now known as Rockwell International. I was a research engineer. My job was to act as liaison between chemical and electrical engineers to supply a chemical informational database. We worked on some of the original stealth bomber strategies.

First of all, they didn't know what to do with me. I was the first black professional employee hired in my position, and have been the first in every major job I've had. It's not bad or good; it was just the sign of the times. I had a run-in with another employee whom I later learned was my boss. Our department had merged with another and in the process there was a realignment of supervisory positions. No one informed me about this change. It probably seemed stupid to me because the issues had nothing to do with my ability to do the job, but the way to go about doing a procedure in which there were no established guidelines. Anyway, they let me go. This was hard on me because I felt I had let my family and my race down. I didn't fail or succeed. I just didn't know the game that was being played.

Work – Applied Research Chemist

My next job was with Dowell, a division of the Dow Chemical Company at the time. Dowell has since become Dowell-Schlumberger. I had a much better time here. It seems they had a meeting before I came and decided to make the best of it. My first few months went so well, it didn't make any difference what they did afterward. I was successful both in their eyes and mine as well. They had an excellent training program for new chemists and by the time I started my own work I had a lot of confidence. By the time I left I had two patents, two national or regional papers published, and more than 12 products developed in the four plus years I was there. With all the success I had, it didn't seem at the time that big to me. It was what I was hired to do. It was, however, the beginning of my best years.

Work – College Professor

My next job was what I considered to be the best job I ever had in terms of quality of life. I had a plan to get a PhD, work in industry for five years and then teach. It almost happened that way. I didn't get a PhD until 20 years later. I taught chemistry at my alma mater, Langston University. It was a great feeling to be surrounded by black people. There was no need to put on a mask; you were free to be yourself. However, I ran into problems politically. One of my main goals was to help students gain some sense of what to expect in the outside world and how to operate there. It worked in the classroom.

Problems occurred when I tried to help a group of students who were considered troublemakers. They were mostly out-of-state students and this was in the 1960s when many students were activists. I wanted to show them how to operate successfully without alienating the administrative powers. I was so concerned about these students that I never considered I would be in jeopardy. I went through the administration every step of the way and eventually got them approved as a recognized organization, The Afro-American Society. I had had experience in organizing as I had helped organized and was the first president of a similar pre-curser group, "The Twentieth Century Society," (the first organization formed by Black students) at the University of Oklahoma, six years before.

The students were ultimately very successful and made many contributions to the school and the Langston community. They made it without me because I was let go as I was considered too much of a threat to the administration. I was told that I would have to go even though my salary was paid for by a grant and I taught at least one course successfully that had never been taught before and another that had not been taught for several years. I was told that if I involved the students in any way the National Guard would be called out. It shocked me because I would have never put the students or the school at risk like that. So, I left.

Work – Program Specialist

I was hired next into the Business and Industrial Services department, the Continuing Educational Center, at the University of Oklahoma. I coordinated, developed and ran management-training programs that were related to minority employees. This job was the best I've had in terms of position, power and money. In this job, you had to make your own monies. After being there a year, I procured a contract through the Office of Minority Business Enterprise of the U.S. Department of Commerce. In fact, it was the first educational and training contract awarded by them. I was doing very well. I had my own department with two budgets, one with hard monies and the other soft monies through contracts.

This job represents the high point of my working career; however, three very strange events occurred. The first was while I was attempting to get a lucrative contract with the Dallas, Texas Police Department to assist them in their efforts to hire and retain more minority policepersons. Just as it seemed they were ready to sign a contract, a police officer accidentally shot a Hispanic boy while trying to scare them into talking about some alleged criminal event. Several days later, a riot broke out, during a demonstration. As a result, the innovative police administration was kicked out and the old guard came in and killed any chance to do our program.

Working - Consulting

The second incident occurred with a local Black activist group in Oklahoma City. At the time, they had developed more than a dozen businesses and wanted my department to help them improve the success of their businesses. Just as we were finalizing the details of the deal, the leader was run out of town and the deal went down the drain.

The third event occurred with a friend of mine from Minnesota. We were negotiating a deal that would have installed me as a training director for a five-state region to help develop and improve minority businesses. I had left the university and formed my own consulting business. And, you might guess, just as we were finalizing the deal, my friend was offered a position she could not refuse. Of course, when she left, the deal fell through.

At this point, I felt snake bitten. Within a year and a half, I was bankrupt, divorced and had no job. I decided that my life was not working and I needed a change. I went underground for five years. This is the period I call my wilderness years, where I recreated myself and initiated the process of becoming Thomas III.

Thomas III

It was during my wilderness years that I began to understand who I really am and could be. It had begun years earlier, when my secretary, Cherie, helped me get books on yoga and astrology. I owe a lot to her for the push she gave me for these times were really difficult. As a result of her influence, I taught myself yoga and thus learned to relax for the first time in my life. That was huge. I mean really huge! I also taught myself how to cast astrology charts and do rudimentary interpretations. Learning astrology began my metaphysical training. I later chose other mediums, because astrology was just too much to deal with at that time. Astrology is as close to being a science in the metaphysical world as chemistry or physics is in the intellectual world. I had had enough of the systematic oriented approaches already. I didn't know it at the time but I wanted a more intuitive path.

Cherie also gave me a couple of books written by Carlos Castaneda. I read a few lines and gave it back, then asked her, "Why did you give me these books about drugs?" When I read them later, I realized they were not about drugs but about a way of living life as a warrior. Castaneda defines a warrior as one who knows life is an illusion but acts as though it is real and makes his or her own choices. That was exactly what I needed, a way of making my own choices because of what I wanted to do; not what was expected by others or my impressions of what others expected of me. In fact, his book, *Journey to Ixtlan, the Lessons of Don Juan*, became my bible of sorts.

At this point in life, I had to remake myself. All those years, I kept fighting my inability to fit in, to conform, to be the all-American kid. I stopped trying to be. In those five years that I termed my wilderness years, I shed most of my religious, political, social and economic orientation. I became spiritual and stopped looking outside of myself for confirmation of who I am and began to look inside. This was no small feat. Once you make that kind of decision the universe tests you in all these areas. You have to have new ways of generating what you want in life. You really must now literally be able to create what you want. So, I now practice the art of creating what I want at any time.

Thomas III - My Call to the Ministry

My call to the ministry came as the result of a series of dreams. As a psychic reader, I also do dream interpretations. I learned dream interpretations from several sources; (1) Gestalt dream interpretations by Frederick Perls; (2) Books on dreaming by Patricia Garfield and Stephen LaBerge; and (3) interpretations by the School of Metaphysics.

Dream One

I dreamt that I was on top of a mountain. I was female and pregnant. My pregnancy was near the end of the third trimester, near to the point of giving birth. There was a man beside me who was trying to push me off the edge. I knew he didn't have the power or strength to push me off as I was the stronger one. However, he kept on pestering me; so, I pushed him off the back edge that wasn't so steep. Just as he fell, I reached down, caught him and pulled him back up before he hurt himself.

Once I awakened, I knew immediately what the dream meant. In most dream interpretation systems, the dreamer creates all portions of the dream from their subconscious mind. Thus, the dreamer is actor, director, scenery, and props, that is, everything in the dream. The female represents my inner consciousness, that part of me that contains the understanding I have achieved in this lifetime and others. The male represents my outer consciousness or conscious mind. The mountain represents the obstacles that I have overcome during my present and previous lifetimes. The pregnancy represents a higher level of consciousness I was about to achieve by overcoming these obstacles. The male trying to push me off is related to the efforts of my conscious mind to be in control. However, my inner consciousness knew that it was better equipped to help me negotiate on the higher level of consciousness. By pushing the conscious mind off the edge, my inner consciousness established control. At the same time, the inner mind had no desire to eliminate the conscious mind. In fact, it realizes that both minds, conscious and inner conscious, are needed to deal with the next level of consciousness. And, only by the two cooperating with each other can I safely reach my goal of becoming one with God, "All That Is."

Dream Two
I dreamt that I was at a religious convention. I was to introduce the speaker. Somehow, I made the speaker angry. Because I made him angry, he told me I had to speak. I said to him, "How can I give a speech? I don't know what to say?" All of a sudden, I was before a "Burning Bush." And I said, "Oh, No! Please not me, I can't do this". At that point, a black dot appeared, and it grew into a black female figure.

This dream is my "Calling Dream." The Burning Bush really got to me, such that it took me more than 15 years to finally accept the call. I did create a church. It's called the First Khametic Church of Gnosticism. I use the term "Khametic" after the word that ancient Egyptians called their land, "Khamit." Gnosticism is the philosophical base for the church, as "Gnosticism" means inner knowing. That is, like my explanation for the Disciple

Thomas, each person must have his or her own personal experience and not go by the experience of others. My church is also a church of one because I don't want a flock. Of course, anyone can belong as long as they have their own center and don't become dependent. I like to define my church experience as a personal ministry.

Dream Three

There were several dreams during the night of my third dream. The kind of dreams that let you know that something very important was coming up. I was outside of a structure that had several doors, about seven. I tried to go through and couldn't open them. After several attempts, as I was trying to open a door, a black female opened it from the other side and then closed it after she passed through. This happened several times with a different black female at each door.

This dream gave me the answer to the appearance of the black female figure in my "Calling" dream. When a male dreams about a female, the female represents aspects of his inner consciousness. The inner consciousness holds the knowledge base of information gained in this lifetime as well as other lifetimes. So, each black female represents a set of understandings in his knowledge base.

All in all, then, the three dreams together helped initiate my path toward my spiritual growth and development. The first dream let me know that my new self would be the future Thomas III, was about to be born. The second dream let me know that I had been called and initiated my ministry to help others. The third dream gave me reference points where I could obtain the information I would need at any given time to do my "work."

Thomas III - Work

In the year 1977–78, three very significant and life changing events occurred. I became bankrupt, divorced and made a life-changing decision about work. I discovered that I was not a good marketer, and just when I thought I was set to expand into new areas, it all fell through. I have previously discussed one of those incidents earlier in the section, The Doubting Thomas – Consulting. I had exhausted all my retirement funds, but was not generating any new monies. I tried to find a job in Minneapolis, since my wife had filed for separate maintenance. However, I realized I couldn't leave my kids and I didn't understand then how I could take a full-time job here or out of town. I realized by this time that although I was very successful as a worker, creating patents, new products, new programs, etc., it just wasn't me. I also found myself, consistently in trouble politically because I couldn't be anybody's "boy." It seemed to me that wherever I went it boiled down to choosing what side I was going to be on. I didn't want to be on any side, I just wanted to work and do my job.

My wife and I got together again; however, two weeks after I filed for bankruptcy some five months later, she filed for a divorced. I knew the marriage was over but I believe in commitments and I also didn't want to leave my kids. When she filed for a divorce, it freed me because she broke the commitment. It was over for me.

A month after my divorce was final I was offered a job with Southwestern Bell as a regional director in the St. Louis, Mo. area. It was a very lucrative offer, but I turned it down. At the time, I was in school with no job, no money at all and no prospects. I knew that I couldn't go back to that system again. For my own sanity, I had to find a new path in life — something that related to me and what I wanted to do in life.

Thomas III - Education

First, I had to redefine myself. I was working on a PhD. The main focus of my earlier classes was the concept of holism, which was defined in terms of the right brain. Well, I couldn't see a half brain being whole, so I wrote a concept paper describing a whole brain philosophy that became the conceptual framework for my dissertation prospectus. This whole brain philosophy became the basis of my personal philosophy and for more than 20 years has helped me to balance seemingly opposing ideas in my head, my work and my life. The underlying framework of this philosophy is shown in the article, "Do I Believe in God" at the beginning of this book.

My work as a PhD candidate served as a time to complete the development of my personal philosophy. I spent 10 years reading, writing, thinking and acting in ways to foster my spiritual development. I even attended "The School of Metaphysics" in Norman, Okla., for nine months. Along with my formal training I was also being trained intuitively.

During the late 1970s, I became interested in the spiritual, metaphysical and psychic world. It was here I found a home, a place that I could grow with few limits. After seven or eight years of study, I became a psychic. The psychic world has provided me with the opportunity to practice and develop the skills I've learned intuitively. I've found a whole new world, far different from the religious and scientific world I grew up in. I know that most people who don't truly understand the psychic world may see it as something in the twilight zone or a 1-900 psychic line. I see the psychic world as a place where I can truly be me, something I've wanted all my life. In this world, truly everything is possible, and more importantly I can develop the whole Thomas.

I have a goal to become one with God consciously and I also seek a path toward an enlightened life. The psychic arena provides me with an opportunity to explore and express this oneness and move toward enlightenment. In this arena I've also found people who are like me, so, I am no longer alone. This body of people contains both my client base and a new set of friends. I've also found within this body an inner circle of friends whose interests are the same as mine if not, very similar. This inner circle of friends has become a second family for me. This network of people, clients, friends and an inner circle of friends forms an arena whose interaction with me has created a sense of synergism. We help each other grow, develop a sense of inner peace, and explore our spiritual connection.

It was during this period I also experimented with marijuana. I know enough from my training as a chemist to stay away from other types of drugs, especially those generated in labs. I know they are far too dangerous. I think it might be helpful to discuss different types of drug users. We live in a drug culture that consists of people who use drugs of all types every day, both legal and illegal. I am not defending drug use. I just want to point out that this culture is hypocritical. On the one hand, we preach "Just Say No! to Drugs." On the other hand, there is a legal drug issue that's overlooked, i.e., alcohol, cigarettes, pharmaceuticals, etc., that are just as bad and sometimes worse. At the same time, there is a so-called war on drugs (an oxymoron to me) that seems to be going nowhere. I must say I am not advocating or condoning the use of drugs. I just want to point out a few inconsistencies. Enough said.

For those who take drugs, I've found that there are three types of users. Type I individuals use drugs recreationally to escape normal realities because it is hard for them to have a good time without the help of cigarettes, alcohol, marijuana, or other drugs of that type. Type II users have trouble dealing with normal realities period, because life is either too painful or they can't cope with the rules of society that don't seem to be made for them. Quite a few groups of indigenous individuals fall in this category all over the world. And then, there is Type III. Type III users use drugs to induce altered states of reality that extend their senses to observe and negotiate life's problems and mysteries. Indigenous people all over the world currently use drugs for this purpose. Some scientists have also used drugs in the same way. In the book, *Center of the Cyclone* by John Lilly, the author discusses how LSD in its purest form is safe. Fortunately or unfortunately, it is only available for research purposes.

During the time I experimented with marijuana, I found I could enter these altered states of reality and access information about the inner Thomas, my environment and the universe that didn't seem to be available under normal conditions. However, once I understood that a particular state was possible or available I learned to reach those states without the use of drugs. You pay a price when you are in an induced state. You really can't be very productive in normal activities of work or dealing with life's problems. Besides it takes several days to come back to normal reality.

Most of these experiences occurred in the early 1980s. That whole decade produced an enriched awareness within me about my relationship with the world. It let me know that there was more to life than just the humdrum of everyday living. There was an exciting world within as well as out there. All in all, it was my next step in developing a working or operational philosophy that became the basis for calling myself, "The Holistic Warrior."

Thomas III – The Holistic Warrior

The Holistic Warrior is defined as the name indicates. Holism refers to the idea that the whole is more than the sum of its parts; one has to determine the relationships between the parts as well, to know the whole. In this case, the parts refer metaphysically to the outer, inner and higher conscious components of me. I must not only understand each component but I must also know and experience how each of the three components relate to each other. See the "The Tree" p. 122; within the spiritual realm I prefer to use outer, inner and higher consciousness to reference the mind states.

Now, a warrior seeks to conquer. In this case, I am not conquering some external foe, but conquering the need for my outer consciousness to be in control. I am working to help my outer conscious mind (the intellect) seek counsel with my inner conscious mind and get the two to work together as one. When the two work together as one, as indicated in the Adam and Eve Story, a new consciousness will emerge, allowing me to go consciously to the next level of evolution.

At this point in my life, I created two different paths. (1) During the week, I work with several governmental agencies and businesses as a management consultant specializing in planning, communication, motivational and team-building programs. (2), on weekends, I travel primarily in the Southwest as well as other parts of the United States, doing psychic readings. As a reader, I am not a "1-900" psychic, although I use the same skills they use.

I consider myself as one who "teaches you how to fish", so you can take care of your own life. I don't want to be responsible for you or anyone else; I have enough trouble taking care of myself. The two paths together keep me sane, allowing me to process information and experiences, develop understanding, and grow as a person. Out of these experiences comes, Thomas III.

Be The Best Of Whatever You Are

If you can't be a pine on the top of the hill,
Be a scrub in the valley- but be
The best little scrub by the side of the rill;
Be a bush if you can't be a tree

If you can't be a bush be a bit of the grass,
And some highway happier make;
If you can't be a muskie then just be a bass-
But be the liveliest bass in the lake!

We can't all be captains, we've got to be crew,
There's something for all of us here,
There's big work to do, and lesser to do,
And the task you must do is the near.

If you can't be a highway then just be a trail,
If you can't be the sun be a star;
It isn't by size that you win or you fail-
Be the best of whatever you are!

-Douglas Malloch

The Many Faces of Thomas III

Previously, I've described the evolution of the three modes of Thomas that ends with the development of Thomas III. Recently, during my 4 a.m. meditation, I was processing how I became a psychic. As I reviewed the different events that led to my choosing this unusual path, I realized that there was another section to be discussed.

There are many faces to Thomas III. I'm reminded of an exercise in a course I've been teaching to state government employees called, "Lateral Thinking." This exercise contains a figure of a cube and asks the question, "Which side of the cube is in front?"

The Cube

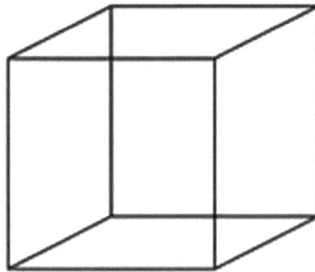

The answer is, "Whatever side you choose to focus on."

The Six-Pointed Star Planning Model

I have a certification in one of the best planning systems, I've seen when it comes to strategic planning. It works very well in the civilized world; however, I don't use this method anymore. As I have made a choice to live life in a balanced way, I use a different system. This system is called, "The Six-Pointed Star Planning Model." The Six-Pointed Star is an ancient symbol found in many cultures (I'll let you research its origins). The most widely known is the "Star of David." The idea came to me because I used the final model from the Holistic Model of the Universe shown on page 31 to form the graphic image on the business cards I use in my spiritual coaching work. It was easy to use this to display the format of my planning model.

The Six-Pointed Star is also used to represent the axiom, "As it is above, so it is below. This axiom appears in the beginning of Emerald Tablets by Hermes Trismegistus. It refers to the idea that the macrocomos is the same as the microcomos.

This model took on greater significance when I discover a six-pointed star in an aura photograph I took several years ago.

> Look at the pictures on the page (203). It is an Aura Photo. Each person has an energy field around them called the "aura." Aura Photo cameras were developed in the early to mid-eighties that captures this field in color form. I have taken many of these photos since 1987. Two years ago, I took a photo after performing a yogi breathing technique, "The Breath of Fire," while sitting in an energized chair for five minutes. I had an aura photo taken immediately afterwards. That photo is shown on the next page. Please look at the area over my heart and find the six-pointed star. Since that time, I have taken at least three more photos with a star over my heart. My understanding is that the display of a six-pointed star over your heart in an aura photo is extremely rare. I will include a section in an appendix of other photos, along with a copy of a logo I use as in my posters.

I use the Six Pointed Star Planning model to periodically set goals. It helps me to have a more comprehensive planning procedure that represents the six most important areas in my life. You might think of it as a metaphysical strategic planning model. Each one of the six sections represents a planning area within itself.

I also use this model to understand the many parts of me. Each section can be used to describe a different set of parts, where each part represents a different face.

Six-Pointed Star Superimposed

of the Holistic Paradigm Logo

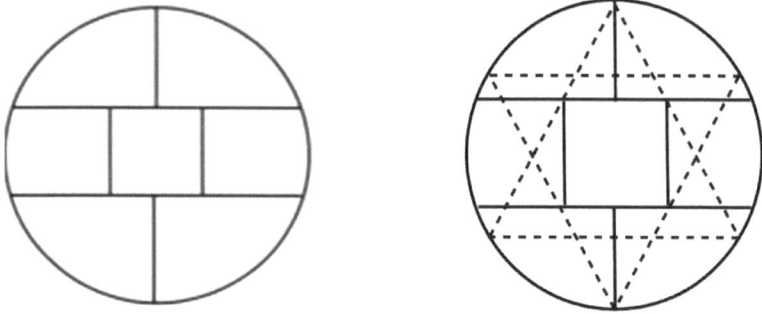

The Six-Pointed Star Planning Model

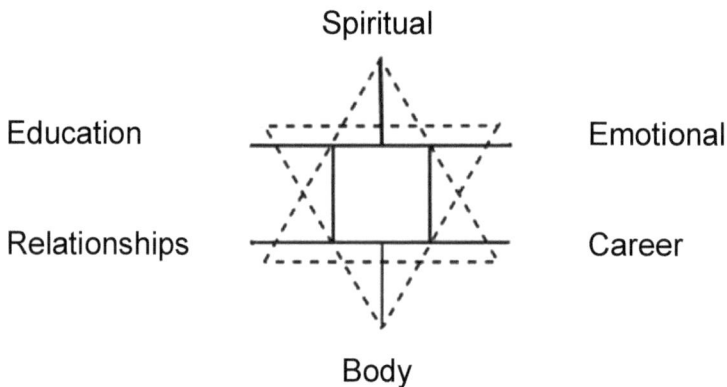

Spiritual

Education

Emotional

Relationships

Career

Body

The many faces of Thomas III can be explained in terms of these planning sections. They are as follows:

Spiritual – The Holistic Warrior, Psychic, Thomas III

Education – Student, Teacher, Observer

Emotional – Determine, The Doubting Thomas, The Raging Bull

Relationships – Father/Grandfather, Husband, Friend

Career – Management Consultant, Psychic, Author

Body – Runner, Overweight, Survivor

There are many other faces, too numerous to list, that have been a part of me over the 70-plus years of my life. It is not just enough to know that I have these faces; all of these faces must be integrated into one. I've been strongly influenced by three philosophers, Gurdjieff, Persig and Castaneda. Gurdjieff was a Greek Armenian philosopher who died in the early 1940s. He developed a complex system of thought, behavior and a psychological framework, usually referred to as "The Work." The chief purpose of "The Work" is to wake you from an unconscious sleep by integrating your many personalities called by Gurdjieff, "The Many I's". Using the analogy of a horse-driven carriage, the question is asked, "Who is driving the carriage?"

Persig has written two books, *Zen and the Art of Motorcycle Maintenance: An Inquiry into Values* and *Lila: An Inquiry into Morals*. The former has become almost a cult book during the past 25 years. Persig seeks to integrate the structure of technology with the creativity of art. He uses a Zen trick of becoming one with the integration process, using the motorcycle as a metaphor for structure and his past personal experiences as a foundation in an attempt to define quality. His book, *Lila*, continues this process and produces a different framework for evaluating quality. Both *Zen* and *Lila* are allegories that present a new reality or a different framework to the world of philosophy. They are written from a "standard reference" but utilize a fresh perspective that allows the reader to evolve along with the storyline itself. In other words, Persig's writings, like Daniel Quinn, Marlo Morgan and others who write about connectivity are "out of the box!" I suspect that many, if not most, mainstream philosophers will have difficulty with his books. His style is like a mosaic tapestry, there are pieces here and there and at first glance, there seems to be no underlying connection until most of the image is formed. The central theme in both books is not separation of a subject/object paradigm but creating a holistic paradigm where both coexist together as one. Again, connectivity is the key.

Castaneda has written many books detailing a continuing story about his 10-year apprenticeship in becoming a metaphysical or spiritual warrior. In his book, *Journey to Ixtlan*, he describes a perception of warriorship. A warrior is one who does not seek to conquer others but rather him- or herself. His process of becoming a warrior follows a path of development from a person of habit, to a hunter, and to a warrior. In this book, he presents a procedure an individual can undergo to become a warrior. An apprentice starts as an individual with many habits and therefore is predictable. When you are predictable you can be controlled and are considered to be prey. By erasing personal history, losing a sense of self-importance, letting death be your advisor, and assuming responsibility for your life you can become a hunter. By becoming inaccessible, disrupting the routines of your life, treating every moment as though it was your last and becoming accessible to the power within you and all life, the hunter becomes a warrior. Thus, this procedure demonstrates the development of an apprentice into a warrior who is impeccable, trusting his or her personal power regardless of whether it is small or enormous.

My knowledge of Gurdjieff's work helps me to understand the necessity of integrating the many parts of me, my many faces. My understanding of Persig's work reinforces my own notion of connecting these faces to form an integrated whole. And my practice of Castaneda's work provides me with a procedure to become a warrior that allows me to act as an integrated whole person.

As I have stated previously, I am on a spiritual journey to know God consciously. The path I've chosen on this journey is that of "The Holistic Warrior." As "The Holistic Warrior," I have the freedom to explore, process, and integrate my experience into a knowledge base that produces a knowing with me. This knowledge base helps me to grow, make sense of the events within my life, and helps others as well. Every event in my life provides an opportunity to grow and evolve, especially when I am able to rise above, because of, or in spite of, the emotional trauma these events may generate. Best of all, I've found the answers and understandings from these events by going within. I believe that the power within me that Castaneda speaks about is God given and God driven, the source of my inner voice. My inner voice guides me in a multitude of ways; 1) through the books I've read or listened to on tape; 2) my interactions with others through my lectures or teachings to students, 3) readings to clients and discussions with friends; 4) my dreams; 5) or just when I'm driving and I let go of having to get there. When I listen to my voice, life is good.

Book Three

The most effective way to live is as a warrior. A warrior may worry and think before making any decision, but once he makes it, he goes on his way, free from worries or thoughts; there will be a million other decisions still awaiting him. That's the warrior's way.

– A Separate Reality, Carlos Castaneda

Where Do I Go From Here?

The Tao of Duality

The last step in the synthesis of Thomas III is to understand how this philosophy can be made applicable to everyday life. Many of the philosophies I've studied in the past were difficult to apply. According to Bertrand Russell, in his book, "A History of Western Philosophy",

> Philosophy can be seen as something intermediate between theology and science. Like theology, it consists of speculations on matters as to which definite knowledge has so far been unascertainable; but like science it appeals to human reason rather than to authority, whether that of tradition or that of revelation. Definite knowledge belongs to science, while all dogma as what surpasses definite knowledge belongs to theology.

Gordon Ziniewicz, in a paper, "Wisdom and Dialectic," has offered a more practical definition. He defines philosophy as:

> A highly individualized affair, tailored to the intellect and temperament of individual people – is a quest for a view of the world as a whole and the place of human beings (including one) within that whole. In this quest, this journey, there is both movement and rest, seeking and stopping for a while. After much experience and thinking, we come to a temporary way-station, a world-view, a perspective, and a "philosophy." After a short stay with opinions that seem valid and fruitful at the time, we once again take to the road – think things over again, revise our opinions, come to new conclusions. New experiences challenge old answers; new suffering revokes old generalizations.

I sought a working philosophy as described in the two definitions above, in my mid to late twenties. I had become disillusioned with Christianity because of my anger with the political, social, and religious structure of the United States. How could a country that considered itself Christian allow slavery? How could the same country when it supposedly freed those slaves, allow a segregated society in the south and a de facto segregated society in its northern regions? How could God-fearing people let this happen? And for that matter, how could God let this happen?

To me, the ills and problems of Negroes (our preference at that time) were directly related to what others people did to us. This theme, that someone was doing evil to Negroes (Blacks) and therefore me, is part of a syndrome that followed me throughout my young adult life. My ex-wife divorced me when I was at my lowest point of existence and took most of what I had. I said to my therapist some years later, "She did it to me." When I observed the effect of Human Relations Conferences on our struggles in the latter days of the Civil Rights Movements, I saw that they were primarily venting sessions while the conditions that most Blacks worked under remained the same. I didn't see changes happening quickly enough, at least the changes I wanted to see. I wanted the ability to fail without it affecting what other Blacks might or might not do in the future (When you are the first Black employee in that position in every Job you've had, you can't fail).

The idea that other people could dictate or determine my future didn't sit too well for me. I was told many times as a youngster that I could do anything I wanted to. I could go as far as I wanted to go. However, by the time, I was in my thirties I was totally disillusioned. I had reached a fairly high point in life. I remember sitting in my recliner chair, of my four bedroom two-story house and saying "I made it." I had a nice house; two great daughters; a marriage that was okay; a great job (I was director of my own program that I created); and I was actively involved in community change.

It went all downhill from there. I lost everything, even my relationship with my daughters, albeit very briefly. A combination of therapy and a new and more wholesome relationship with my daughters changed everything. Instead of seeing what people did to me; I sought to determine what kind of decisions I made to put myself in that position; to determine the consequences of the decisions I made. Doing so, freed me. It allowed me to make decisions that were in my own best interests regardless of the circumstances. It gave me a working formula to deal with both personal and world blocks. This event gave birth to "Thomas III."

The synthesis of Thomas III seeks a foundation that allows me to become a fully functioning being, working on a path toward enlightenment, "The Path of the Holistic Warrior." The next two chapters describe the foundation of my journey along this path. It seeks to define a system that continually allows me to make "Conscious – Deliberate – Choices" along my path and by doing so, "I can choose a Path with a Heart!"

Two Paths To Spirituality

The mid-to-late seventies was a very traumatic period for me. It was a period of transition, a transition from a time when my life was based primarily on a belief in the viability of the American dream. I strove to achieve all my goals and for the most part achieved them. I was very successful in all the endeavors I attempted, even though at the time I didn't put too much stock in those achievements. Recently, I've spoken of that time in my life as the "Young Lions" period. On the one hand it was great and wonderful, however, on the other hand it was not very fulfilling. I wasn't very happy because it didn't seem to make a difference in the over-all scheme of things.

The events that led up to and embraced this transition occurred in three periods; 1) The Model Cities Period, where my passion led to a career; 2) Human Relations Period, where I discovered I didn't want to be labeled; and 3) Wilderness Years Period, where I discovered who I am and who I wanted to be. All three periods were based on my activities as a volunteer. They are a tribute to an old adage, "When you do what you really like doing regardless of whether or not you are paid for your efforts, money will follow", and so it did for me.

Model Cities Period

The first of these events occurred at the height of the Civil Rights movement. This was a period of protest, change, and promise. In my early years in Tulsa, I had an opportunity to be a part of the Tulsa's Model Cities Program. One of my best friends, Curtis Lawson, was Tulsa's first Black Representative to the state legislature. He got me appointed to the original Model Cities Planning Commission. When the City of Tulsa was selected, I became a volunteer to work with the Target Area Action Group, a citizen-action group that served as the focal point for change or renewal. I didn't live in the "Target Area" (an area designated by the city that served as the place for change to take place). My volunteer efforts were focused mainly in the areas of organizing and conducting meetings. I had learned to plan and run meetings during my pledge period as a Sphinxman of Alpha Phi Alpha Fraternity, Inc. All of our meetings both during the pledge period and as a member of the fraternity were conducted according to Robert's Rules of Order. They were very well organized and well run. I was able to utilize this experience in other meetings as well during my college days.

The goal of the Model Cities Program was to change and/or upgrade the lifestyles and socio-economic status of its residents. It is my assessment that the Model Cities Program, like many or most of the poverty programs of that period had lofty goals but didn't quite meet their targets. There were many reasons why these programs were not as successful as they could have been. For instance,

1. Residents were not use to power sharing, which resulted in a lot of disruptions which seriously limited their effectiveness;

2. Residents did not know how to empower themselves to facilitate the change process.

3. The City of Tulsa was not truly committed to making the internal changes in attitudes and power sharing.

4. Residents were not in the long-term or even short-term planning loop for construction activities and job availabilities. And so, did not have relevant information needed in a timely manner.

5. There were not enough industrial and business commitments to help residents improve and maintain their socio-economic status.

You might get the idea that on the surface, the powers that be wanted change but underneath they wanted things to stay the same. I experienced this same attitude during the Human Relation Conferences held in the 1970s. They were great at allowing participants to vent their anger and frustrations but nothing seemed to change afterward. Don't get me wrong, I benefited from these experiences; as did many people like me.

And many of us also helped train a lot of people and facilitate efforts to pull ourselves up by our bootstraps so to speak. There is a strong Black middle class now as a result of these actions. However, it seems to me that the more things changed the more they stayed the same. Look at the areas in Black communities now that haven't been taken over by urban renewal to make way for "downtown" expansions, etc.

Human Relations Period

This period of transition also served as the foundation of my renaissance years. I was even called a "Renaissance Man" once while being introduced as the closing speaker at my first human relations labor-management conference held at the University of Oklahoma in the summer of 1970. This speech served as an interview for a job as a Program Development Specialist II (a position designed to develop, coordinate, and present management training workshops for business supervisors). My interviewer wanted to know how well I could perform, impromptu. It was to be a fifteen-minute speech, so I wrote a five-minute speech that night before and was going to ad lib the rest. Prior to my presentation, the speaker before me went way over his time allotment. I was asked by the workshop presenter to condense my speech to five minutes. I presented the speech in an eloquent and succinct manner. I didn't know I had that in me because that was my first real speech of that type. I got a standing ovation and was later told by the presenters that that was the best fifteen-minute speech condensed to five minutes they ever heard. I never told them that five-minutes was all the time I had prepared for. Needless to say, I got the job.

There were many other experiences that were significant during my renaissance period, such as my subsequent tenure as a Program Development Specialist II. This was a unique job because it was part of the Oklahoma Center for Continuing Education (OCCE) at the University of Oklahoma. Most, if not all, jobs in the OCCE were not funded by the University of Oklahoma. Each department or unit had to create its own funds by selling programs or workshops to private businesses, etc. or by obtaining government contracts. My specialty was to develop and present management training programs with an emphasis on involving minority groups. I became one of the sponsors of the Human Relations Labor-Management Conferences. I developed programs geared toward supervising minority employees. And, I received the first educational and training grant funded by the Office of Minority Business Enterprise, the US Department of Commerce. As a result, for seven years, I had my own department and two operating budgets.

This time was also the post-Civil Rights period when Blacks and other minority groups were just beginning to feel their oats. It was indeed a learning experience for all of us. For me, it was the realization that there has to be another way. Because on the surface it seemed that everything was in order, it was going to be all right; however, underneath I knew something was wrong. It took me a few more years to find out what it was.

There was another problem. Many of us were also labeled as affirmative action workers who didn't get there because of our abilities. We got there because of laws or some political correctness efforts. It seems that we were not qualified to do our jobs no matter how successful we were. So, after 14 years of employment as an engineer, chemist, college professor and department head, I decided to leave this arena and seek a different venue. I no longer wanted to be identified as an affirmative action or any other similar stereotyped worker. I find people who talk against affirmative action programs to be hypocrites because I have seen white workers "affirmative-acted" in companies throughout my working life. Whites who were not as qualified are constantly hired or promoted ahead of more qualified minority workers to this day. I find this dichotomy very interesting.

I wanted to be accepted on my own merits — not because someone put me there. I left that world and began developing my own system, my own way. This period served as the prelude to my wilderness years. I decided I didn't want to work as a regular employee again. I went underground and left everything behind

— professional life, society, religion — all those institutions that seemed to place limitations on me. And at the same time, I also sought to determine the limitations I had placed on myself.

Wilderness Years Period

I spent five years searching for that special sense of who I could be. This was a very special and perhaps the most significant period of my life so far up to that time. During the Wilderness Years, I averaged an annual income of $3,400. It was a period where I've felt the freest. I frequently traveled across the middle of the U.S. from Norman, Okla., to St. Louis, Detroit, Chicago, Minneapolis, Denver and Santa Fe, N.M. Some trips were made to a set of cities like Minneapolis and Detroit or to Denver and Santa Fe. Many were just to Santa Fe or Denver alone. I went skiing, backpacking and camping. All of these trips were made in a Karman Ghia, a sports model Volkswagen that was 10-years-old when I bought it from a friend. I flew on trips to San Francisco, and Washington, D.C. All of the trips were made while I was making $3,400 a year. I'm amazed when I think of that period.

During the summers, I traveled with my two daughters, Michelle and Nikki. Most of our trips were to track meets. Michelle was a power runner like me, and Nikki was the speedster and all-around athlete. We went to many AAU track and field meets all over the southwest. The three of us would pile in the Karman Ghia and take off.

It was during this period that I learned to trust. Most of the experiences with trust occurred while driving the Karman Ghia, such as,

1. Driving from Minneapolis to Denver without a starter. I was headed to Denver anyway. It was the weekend and when I'm ready to leave a place, I want to go right then. I had just bought the car from a friend. He had just gone out of town and as I attempted to leave Minneapolis, the starter went out. So, I left anyway. Whenever I stopped, I made sure I stopped if possible on a hill. Sometimes I rolled down and forgot to turn on

the ignition. Regardless of what happened, whenever I needed help someone was there to give me a push.

2. The car's gas gauge didn't work. I measured the amount of gas by the car's mileage. I rarely ran out of gas, but when I did there was always someone there to give me a lift.

3. Driving from Minneapolis to Norman without brakes. My brakes went out in Minneapolis and the Volkswagen service department wanted to charge me an exorbitant amount to repair the brakes. I refused because I knew my mechanic back in Norman would charge me not more than $200. So, I signed a release form and they rigged my emergency brake to work as my braking system. I knew I had to be very careful and obviously I made it home.

4. Driving from Emporia, KS to Norman without a clutch. My daughters had an AAU Regional Track Meet at the University of Kansas. On the way home that Saturday night, as we approached the turnpike gate at Emporia, my clutch went out. We were towed to a motel. There was a Ward's Auto Department in a shopping center across the street. The next morning, the service person at Ward's couldn't fix the car. So, to keep from waiting until Monday morning, he showed me how to shift the gears by listening to the sound of the engine. You can't do that with the cars we have now. Of course, I made it home without harming the gears.

5. I left Santa Fe one trip and 50 miles later, about five miles from Las Vegas, N.M., I ran out of gas. I found out after being towed that my gas tank had a hole in it and there was no one who knew how to fix it. The service person told me he knew of a wanderer who just happened to be in town and he was the only one who could possibly fix my car. Everything worked out of course.

167

There were many other experiences besides the ones I've discussed. As a result, I learned to trust my feelings. I further believe this period was a training ground for my current career as a psychic. Before that period, I considered my feelings to be my weakness. I've always had the ability to cry and have been very sensitive. This sensitivity was not something to be proud of because both male and females tend to think badly of men who cry too easily, so they will ostracize you in one way or another. So, I hid this part of me. I now understand that this sensitivity is the source of my strength as well as connected to my "Inner Voice".

Development of My Current Philosophy

My inability to deal with my sensitivity was also due to my inner conflicts about religion and philosophy. At that time, there seemed to be no systems within life that practiced what they preached. Everyone seemed to be out for him or herself. I have always been amused when athletes thank God for being on their side. I wonder does God take sides. You mean God doesn't work for all of us? If God were not neutral how else could we have free will?

I did find something and to my surprise it wasn't a new system. In fact, it was older than most of the institutions or systems I had left. This system was based on spiritually where one sought God, happiness, wealth and harmonious relationships by looking within first. Upon looking within, I found a way to make a connection by establishing a relationship:

1. With the inner part of me; that part that knows how to make life decisions that is in my best interest.
2. With that part of me that knows how to deal with anything and everything. It is the part of me that I consider to be my connection with God.
3. With others around me to create harmonious relationships.
4. With my environment to create the things I want or need in life.

I asked, "Why am I just now finding this system of spiritually?" I realized that it is a choice one has to come or evolve to." In a dualistic system, you can't know the good if you don't know the bad. You can't completely know what you want unless you know what you don't want.

The key to the spiritual system is connecting: Connecting with self, God, others and your environment. This way of life is contrary to all the things I've been taught and even better because I can practice what I teach. This way of life has led me on a journey where I have discovered a different way of looking at my world. A world where I can fit in and not feel like an outsider. And, what's more, I found other people like me and I no longer feel alone. These people are now my friends whom I can talk to without pulling punches or having to explain everything I say; people who are unquestioningly open to and accepting of me.

I also found another system of work and study, the spiritual world. The spiritual world is full of information about the universe that you can't find in the civilized world; at least it's not legitimized. Now, I'm not putting down the understandings I gained from the civilized world down. In fact, I don't want to give up everything I've learned and studied, I want to incorporate what I've learned with the new information I am obtaining from the spiritual world that will allow me to create a balance between the two worlds. The prospectus I wrote for my dissertation gave me just that opportunity to create that balance. As a result, I was able to develop a program that integrated the best of both worlds and helped me function as a whole person. The system I developed, the Holistic Model of the Universe is shown in the first article, "Do I believe in God?"

Years ago, while teaching courses in both chemistry and psychology, I was told that it wasn't possible to teach courses in chemistry and psychology at the same time. First of all, I was already doing it, and second, if I was operating within the context of the civilized world mindset, I might have agreed with him. However, I was operating within the context of the spiritual world where all things are possible since there is no separation between

169

different components of the spiritual world. According to the Holistic Model of the Universe, there is no separation because all components are connected or related to each other.

Two Worlds:
Connectedness and Separateness

In the previous section, we discussed the evolution of my identity as an individual. Since an individual does not operate in a vacuum, he or she must therefore operate among others. Most of our difficult experiences in life come from these interactions or our thoughts about them. The experiences we have with each other sometimes become difficult, troublesome or immersed in conflict because each one of us has our own wants and needs. And, as we seek to satisfy these needs and they become blocked, conflicts and/or difficulties arise. Although these wants and needs may be satisfied by our own efforts, most must be satisfied through our interaction with others. Whether or not these interactions are difficult or troublesome depends on what type of games we play with each other.

As I see it, there are two basic games we can play (1) win-lose and (2) win-win. These games have evolved from a system described in a previous article, "Do I believe in God"? In that article, I discussed a concept of God offered by Walsh in his book, *Conversations with God*. His concept of God proposes that God, in order to know experience, split itself into two parts. One part was based on the concept of love or connection and the other based on fear or separation. Therefore, we can see that the win-lose game is derived from the fear paradigm and the win-win game is derived from the love paradigm.

Separateness: Fear (Win-Lose)
Occupants of a system based on fear view themselves as separate from everything in the universe. They see the universe in hierarchical terms as it relates to their survival; therefore, one group is more important than another. So, the more intelligent they are, the more they may see themselves as superior to everything else. And if they are superior to everything else, then they may feel in charge of everything else. They see every other group in their environment as existing to serve their needs. They also see the universe as having limited resources. Therefore, in

order to satisfy their needs, they must dominate, control or exploit their environment in order to get what they want.

Since they will also see themselves as separate from each other, as they deal with each other, they feel someone must be in control; someone must lead and make the decisions. And, if that's the case, some designated person must be in control. In many cases, that person in control might as well be them or someone they approve of. If this is not so they will not give their allegiance to that person. As they seek to meet their wants and needs, they see everything in terms of win-lose; there is always a winner and a loser and of course they want to be on the winning side. They also see competition as the best way to accomplish their personal or group goals. This is the game played consciously or unconsciously, by most of the people who operate in the civilized world.

Connectedness: Love (Win-Win)

Occupants of a system based on love view themselves as connected to, and thus a natural part of, everything in the universe. They see the universe in hierarchical terms at it relates to a complexity but that any group is equal in importance to any other group. The more understanding they achieve, the more they see themselves as having a responsibility to maintain their connection with themselves as well as other groups. They understand that everything must survive off of other things in their environment but that each group has an equal endowment to survive. When they must satisfy their needs for food or shelter, they honor the beings whose life they must take to satisfy these needs. The universe is abundant and has unlimited resources, therefore there is no need to dominate, control or exploit everything in their environment. They know that what they take will live on as a part of their life and will therefore only take what they need at any time. They know that one day they will serve that same role for something else. They also see the universe as providing everything they need to live, grow, procreate and evolve.

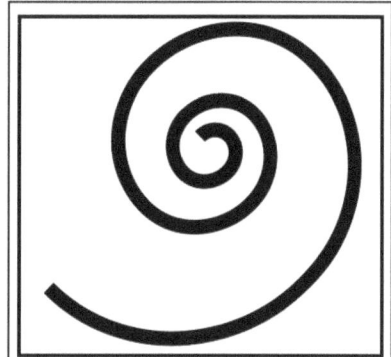

CONNECTEDNESS *Love*	SEPARATION *Fear*
Connecting Win-Win Give and Receive Get Energy from Self Connection Multiple Choices (All good)	Domination, Control, Exploitation Win-Lose Give or Receive Get Energy from Others Attachment Few Choices (may not be good)

How the Current World Operates

There are very few cultures left on this planet that still play by the win-win set of rules. They have been overrun; annihilated, or absorbed by the culture I will call the civilized world or Civilized Matrix. The Civilized Matrix now covers most of the planet. Although there are many variations of political, social and economic subsystems within this matrix, practically all of its participants consciously or unconsciously play the win-lose game.

Most indigenous cultures, which I shall call the Life Matrix, I believe, play the win-win game with others and their environment. It is not to say that they are perfect. They have to obtain food and shelter from their environment as well as protect themselves just as those who live in the Civilized Matrix must do. However, the common element among those in the Life Matrix is that they see themselves as part of their environment and attempt to be in harmony with it. Their attitudes lead them to different decisions about how they interact with their world. They do not seek to exploit, dominate or control their environment but seek to remain in harmony with it. They accept what the environment gives them without destroying it.

For the most part, they have been overrun or absorbed by the Civilized Matrix. As this has happened, many, perhaps most have little or no idea about the ways one survives in the Civilized Matrix. It is difficult for them to play win-lose games and win. As a result, many live in squalor, become alcoholics, are un- or underemployed, or just seem lost. I perceive that as long as the two matrices hold to similar patterns of interacting with each other as they have during the past couple hundred years, these problems will persist.

Now, as much I respect or like the Life Matrix, I don't want to romanticize this matrix. I don't want to live under the same conditions most of them do. I like the comforts as well as the technological advances made in the Civilized Matrix. Actually, I want the best of both worlds. That is, I want the comforts and technological advances of the Civilized Matrix without destroying the environment, and I want to maintain the relationships between the individual, God and the environment as seen in the Life Matrix. Therefore, I am proposing a third matrix that I shall call The Balanced Matrix. It is as follows:

"How Do I Live A Balanced Life?"

1. Become one with God, consciously
2. Grow and evolve into higher levels of consciousness
3. Obtain and maintain peace, optimum health and prosperity
4. Let go of limiting thoughts, behaviors and emotions
5. Obtain and maintain healthy relationships

6. Maintain a dynamic and ecological balance with my community
7. Help others (with their permission) find their way and be of service to the universe and themselves

To live the balanced life, I must be able to live in both worlds since the Civilized Matrix occupies most of the earth. One of the main ways I have been able to maintain my sanity is through my work. My work is divided into two parts: during the week I am management trainer, and on the weekends I am a psychic reader.

Management Trainer

As a management trainer, I conduct workshops on communication, motivation and planning, etc. I seek to help employees, supervisors and managers in local, state and federal government to be better workers and provide better services to their citizenry. I also work with business and industry to help them become more effective and efficient, therefore, producing better products to maximize profits. I really enjoy being in the classroom.

One of the main avenues I use to help organizations provide better services or products is by teaching and demonstrating the art of connecting. I believe when employees in any organization, whether government or industry, are able to buy into the mission and vision of their organization, they form natural connections with that organization as well as with the people who are part of that organization. When a worker, manager or otherwise feels connected to an organization, they see every experience in terms of how it's going to help him or her; not how it hurts them. Then these employees can use whatever skills, abilities and training that are available to them to provide the best possible service or products.

Psychic Reader

In the psychic arena I am able to put all my training and skills into action as well continually work on my own spiritual development. I conduct readings and workshops for both individuals and groups. I am able to help these clients by showing them how to identify their own problems, as well as, personal and emotional blocks, and ~~then~~ find solutions; and develop spiritually. Ultimately, it helps each individual take responsibility for improvement of his or her life.

As I help others, I also help myself. However, I only help those clients whom I have permission. I seek spiritual enlightenment. It is my desire to be one with God, consciously and cross over into the next world with the knowledge and understanding I've gained in this life. I don't want to go through the pain of remembering who I am. Such that, in my next life, I will be free to explore the glory of "All That Is."

Many times I've gained insight and understandings about my own path in life as I helped others come to some resolution about their path. I also am able to gain insight and understanding while traveling to these events. Most of the readings and workshops I've presented are out of town. I travel to these events by car. During these trips in the car, I am able to reach a clear state of altered consciousness. My conscious mind controls the car. So, when I relax and let go of "having to get there," I'm free to communicate with my inner consciousness. It's during these times, along with my 4:00 a.m. meditation that I am able to obtain insights into the problems of my life, past, present or future as well as spiritual guidance. I can ask questions on any topic and get answers; revise or develop new ideas; create lectures or speeches spontaneously; or just be open to whatever information that might pop up at the time.

I've found that when I'm only working in the management arena or in the psychic world, life is more chaotic, difficult or out of balance. However, when I am doing both, the management arena during the week and the psychic world during the weekends, my life is much smoother and in balance. The idea of being in both worlds is nothing new to me, as I have lived most of my life in this manner. As I prepared my dissertation prospectus, I chose to develop a system that was built on a balance between the biomedical and holistic models of health. This idea was spawned from my interest in right and left-brain thought patterns. Holistic health was touted as being right brain oriented. This seemed to be a contradiction to me because I couldn't see half a brain being a whole. So, I developed a system that combined both sides of the brain into a working model. It was from this process, I used as the philosophical underpinning for everything I do, experience, or process.

The "Balanced Life" then, is based on my need to create a balance in all phases of my life, physically, mentally, emotionally and spiritually. That is what this book is all about.

Warriors must be impeccable in their effort to change, in order to scare the human form and shake it away. After years of impeccability, a moment will come when the human form cannot stand it any longer and leaves. That is to say, a moment will come when the energy fields contorted by a lifetime of habit are straightened out. A warrior gets deeply affected, and can even die as a result of this straightening out of energy fields, but an impeccable warrior always survives.

– The Second Ring of Power, Carlos Castaneda

Conclusion
Epilogue: Walking The Walk

In May 2000 I had a third biopsy taken from my prostate. Eleven years before, while going through a physical exam at the University of Oklahoma Health Sciences Center (I was a graduate student at the time), I was sent to an urologist. After an examination, he informed me that I was at risk for prostate cancer. My PSA was between four and five. I knew very little about prostate cancer at the time and I needed to stay aware of the possibilities. He further informed me that black males have the highest incidence of prostate cancer of any other male group in the world. As a result of this encounter, I began to find out everything I could about prostate cancer; and over the next few years had regular exams also began to take several herbs and herbal formulations, such as, Saw Palmetto and Nature Sunshine's PSII formula.

Over the next 11 years I had three biopsies. The first one was the most painful procedure I had ever encountered. If there is something worse than that I pray I never have to deal with it. My third biopsy occurred two years after my second one and the result came back positive. My urologist wanted to perform surgery immediately to deal with the problem. I knew there was no way I wanted surgery. The side effects as well as six weeks recovery period were much more than I wanted to handle. I had already heard about the possible consequences of side effects on my sex drive and other problems. The six weeks recovery would have been disastrous for my business interests.

I was totally shocked by the results of the biopsy because my previous indicators all pointed to a negative result. I was confident that the results would be negative because I had a strong heart feeling during the biopsy procedure, afterward and even when I was informed that the test results were positive.

The reader might remember that I have discussed my reliance on my heart feelings previously in this book. However, after receiving the results from the biopsy and for several months afterward, I was in a state of quandary. If I can't rely on my heart feelings, then what can I trust? I spent that period really searching for answers. I decided on three courses of action: 1) to participate in the brachytherapy treatment program; 2) to work on what I believed to be the root causes of my problem; and 3) to seek the services of a Mongolian Doctor, who had been trained in Tibetan and Chinese medicine.

These three courses represent a balanced approach to the healing process. A balanced approach to healing is based on the recommendations that came as a result of my dissertation prospectus done 20 years earlier. The brachytherapy treatment program represents the traditional biomedical approach; working on the root causes of my problems represents the self-healing approach; and Chinese medical procedures represent the non-traditional or holistic medical approach.

The Brachytherapy Treatment – The Traditional Medical Approach

Since I didn't want surgery, my urologist, told me about the brachytherapy treatment program. Brachytherapy is an advanced cancer treatment program. Radioactive seeds are placed in the tumor itself, giving a high radiation dose to the tumor area while reducing the dosage to the surrounding healthy tissue in the body. The efficacy of the treatment very nearly matches the results of surgery but side effects are greatly minimized with little or no down time at work. My urologist preferred performing surgery to deal with cancer problems, so when I made a decision to use the brachytherapy treatment, he referred me to his partner, who specialized in radiological treatments.

The brachytherapy treatment program can be structured in several treatment forms. My biopsy results showed that I had a Gleason score of 7 out of a top score of 10. Rating the cancerous cells in two areas according to the growth of the cells and adding them together produces this score. Based on these results, my doctor recommended a three-step treatment plan, including:

1. Hormone treatments – To effectively place the radioactive seeds the prostate must be shrunk. This process not only prepares the prostate but attacks the cancerous cells as well. The patient is given one shot and pills once a day over a three-month period until the prostate shrinks to the proper size.

   When the prostate has shrunk to the proper size, a probe is inserted into the patient's anus to map the prostate. This map is used to determine the quantity and placement of the seeds.

2. Radiation Treatments – 25 straight working days of radiation treatments at higher than the normal dosage.

3. Radioactive Seed Implantation.

The medical treatment program, which occurred over a nine-month period, included the above three steps. The results of this treatment program are as follows:

1. Hormone treatments – I chose the hormone, Zoladex, because according to my doctor, even though it was more expensive it had fewer potential side effects. I took Zoladex for two or three periods (from September to March) and had two shots.

   My prostate shrank to the proper size by March 2001. The mapping of my prostate occurred during the second week of March. The mapping procedure was one of the most painful procedures I've experienced since my first prostate biopsy in 1988.

2. Radiation Treatments – this treatment started the first week of April and ended the first week of May. I received a treatment every work-day morning during this period.

3. Radioactive Seed Implantation – The seeds were placed during an outpatient visit the second Friday of May 2001. The procedure went very smoothly. I

remember being placed on the operating table and woke up a couple hours later. It was completed.

Side Effects – Experienced the following:

1. Side effects in January 2001 - began having hot flashes and continued experiencing them until September 2001.
2. Emotional swings - lasted January through the August of 2001.
3. Weight gains – gained more than 35 total pounds; fortunately I had lost approximately 20 pounds before I started the treatment program. I have since gained 20 pounds.
4. Sexual dysfunctions - increased over a period of several months.
5. Urination problems - primarily from the seed implantation. I started taking Flomax tablets a week before the seed implantation. I continued taking Flomax until August 2001.
6. Swelling - in my lower leg and foot.
7. Tiredness and depression - depression continues today though not as strongly as it was in the middle stages of the treatment program.
8. Minor problems - sharp pains that occurred around the left or right side of my midsection, itching, swelling in my face, and soreness here and there.

Self-Healing Approach I – Removing Emotional Blocks

To work on the root causes of my problem, I used a process I had developed years before called, "Heal the Woolies of Your Life." A Woolly represents an unwanted pattern, behavior or emotional block that is embedded within your subconscious mind. The healing process is as follows:

1. Select the appropriate word or phrase that represents the pattern or behavior you want to focus on. You can obtain this word or phrase from any number of sources, such as, Louise Hay's Book,

"You Can Heal Your Life," reading, meditation or any other sources available to you.

2. Repeat the words or phrase over and over again within your mind, like repeating a mantra during meditation.

3. After some time, another word or phrase will pop into your mind. At that point, use this new word as your focus point.

4. Repeat this process over and over again until a picture of some representation of the core of the pattern or behavior presents itself.

5. Keep repeating the word or phrase until you expose what's behind the picture or what's underneath or within the core.

6. At some point, sooner or later, in this process a smile, grin or sigh of satisfaction will appear on your face. The smile, grin or sigh of satisfaction indicates a release has occurred or the core of the problem has diffused and evaporated.

7. Start the process again with a new word or phrase.

I used this process for approximately two and half months. According to Louise Hay's book, *You Can Heal Your Life,* the prostate represents the masculine principle and prostate problems represent (1) mental fears that weaken masculinity and (2) sexual pressure and guilt. I related these issues to my relationships with women. I've had fears about women and have had difficulty connecting with women until my present relationship. Most of these difficulties occurred before the age of 40.

I worked on healing these relationships. I worked on this problem before going to bed and again when I woke up during the night. Information about a given relationship would come to me in a dream or during meditation. I repeated the above procedure until no further information appeared.

Self-Healing Approach II – Healing Mantras

Healing can also be facilitated with sound systems. The sound system I used was the use of mantras.

The word mantra comes from the Sanskrit roots manas (mind) and trai (device). It has come to mean "spiritual sound formula," "that which, when contemplated and repeated, will offer protection."

The proper study of Sanskrit mantras includes physical anatomy; the system of subtle channels in the body; diagrams of spiritual energy processing centers (chakras); and the human voice, which powerfully influences all of the above. Sanskrit mantras are also key to techniques for awakening kundalini, a subtle power cell located at the base of the spine.

The recommended amount and time periods are as follows:

Chant the mantra 108 times twice a day

Repeat this process for 40 days

It is recommended that the mantra is repeated a total of 125,000 times.

I chose two mantras.

Om Shrim Maha Lakshmiyei Swaha ("Om and salutations. I invoke the great principle of great abundance.")

Om Arkaya Namaha ("Om and salutations to the Shining One who removes afflictions.")

The above information was obtained from a CD entitled *Healing Mantras* by Thomas Ashley-Farrands.

I repeated these mantras, using a string of 108-prayer beads as a focal point, for more than a year 80,000 repetitions each.

Chinese Medical Practices – An Alternative Medical Approach

After deciding to undergo the brachytherapy treatment, I still wasn't satisfied. I chose the brachytherapy treatment program because I didn't want to deal with either the effects of surgery or the recovery time required to heal. However, choosing the brachytherapy treatment didn't eliminate side effects, it just minimized them. I had listened to a cassette program on Chinese medicine called *Chinese Secrets of Health and Longevity*. I was intrigued to say the least, particularly with the idea of obtaining noninvasive strategies for maximum energy, lifespan and a practical prescription for total wellness.

A friend in Dallas had told me about a Mongolian practitioner, Dr. Dashima Dovchin, who was trained in Tibetan and Chinese medicine. This doctor specialized in cancer problems and had been brought to the Dallas area from Mongolia by one of her patients. My friend strongly recommended that I see her, so I made an appointment. Upon my first visit, I knew I had made the right decision. My visit with her was inspiring. For once, a doctor connected with me; I knew with her help I would be all right.

Dr. Dovchin, Dashima, as her patients call her, confirmed my concerns about surgery. In my initial visit, she took my pulse for approximately 15 minutes; first my right wrist, then my left wrist, both wrists at the same time, and then my right wrist again. Afterward she said my body was not in good enough condition to recover properly from the effects of surgery. My lungs, kidneys and liver were not in good condition. She was not just talking about my individual lungs, kidneys and liver but the lungs, kidneys and liver as systems within themselves. We spent the next two months improving each of these systems and bringing them back to a better homeostatic balance.

At each visit, I would bring a list of the current side effects I was experiencing. Dashima would in turn use a combination of acupuncture, cups, diet changes or herbs to bring my body system to a better homeostatic balance. As a result of these treatments, I never missed a day of work and I believe I was generally able to function at higher level than I would have been without the treatments. I made office visits once a week for more than a year and a half until most of my side effects subsided.

At this point, Dashima began dealing with my other health issues, such as, allergies, arthritis and weight problems. (I had lost the weight I gained as a result of the medical treatments.) We are currently working on these issues.

Current Health Status

All in all, I am in very good shape with respect to the post-cancer stage. I have been cancer free for more than ten years. I have checkups once a year. My PSA test has been less than 0.1 for more than ten years and I plan to keep it that way. I also still see my doctor of Chinese medicine every three to four weeks to remain in good health.

My health goals include: 1) continually improving my physical health, 2) achieving my weight goals, 3) maintaining a consistent regimen of exercise and 4) keeping the mental and spiritual aspects of myself in balance. As I can achieve and maintain these goals as well as make some improvement here and there, I believe my body will be able to respond appropriately to whatever challenges that are ahead for me.

Physical Fitness

My main goal has been and is now to get my body back in shape. It was a most difficult task during the cancer treatments. Minor problems like "ingrown toenail" have kept me from exercising on a regular basis. In my 40s, when I missed several days of exercise, it was easy to resume my routine and not miss a step. However, when I miss more than two days of my routine; it seems as though I am starting all over again. In order to get fit, I set fitness goals to be able to consistently exercise three to four days a week and bring my weight down to 215 pounds or less.

Fortunately, before I started the treatment programs, I lost 20 pounds by exercising on a regular basis, three to five times a week using the Tae Bo exercise program and a treadmill over a six-month period. I didn't change my eating habits during this period. I achieved my goal of 215 pounds.

As a result of the medical treatments over the next year, I gained approximately 25 pounds. Just before I started the medical part of the treatment, I got very sick. I stopped exercising on a regular basis and did not to get back in an exercise groove for almost ten years.

About six years after I completed the medical treatments, my wife and I went on the South Beach diet. I lost 20 pounds in the first three months but over the next four years my weight fluctuated between 220 and 225 pounds. So, ten years after I completed the medical treatments, I restarted the Tai Bo routine and was able to maintain that routine for a year and half and achieved my goal of maintaining 215 plus or minus 3 pounds. My new goal is 200 pounds.

It has taken me a year and a half to reach the same physical condition I achieved in six months in the previous training period ten years ago. Furthermore, after the year and a half conditioning period, I had to end it because my efforts were too vigorous. So, now I have started a different program on my recumbent bike and I also intend to add a Tai Chi program as well. My weight now is around 211 pounds, plus or minus 3 pounds.

All in all, I am in good condition at this time.

Emotional Challenges: The Story Body (Critical Voice)

My current focus is to focus on "Living in the Now." These past ten years have also been one of the most difficult emotional periods of my life. It has presented me with an opportunity to clear years of emotional residue that caused in a huge buildup of blocked energy. Releasing this energy evidently has been a prerequisite to the next step in my spiritual development. This next step in my spiritual development has been filled with emotional challenges. I apparently was ready to confront some of the life lesson issues I've had difficulty dealing with since childhood.

These challenges include 1) accepting myself, 2) taking care of people, and 3) misplaced focus of attention. All of these challenges have been presented to me during the past year. As a result, I've been continually dealing with or been wrapped up in my "Story Body." Some of you may recognize the Story Body as the "Pain Body" identified by Eckhart Tolle. I called it the Story Body because it relates to a previous paper I wrote about how stories control our lives. This paper was written at the end of 2010. At the end of the year for the past few years I have written papers that represent a summary of my experiences or understandings for that year or as a salute to the coming year. I am including a copy of that paper as an addendum to this book.

The Story Body is a composite of data and emotions that are derived from the events, issues and activities we have experienced as well as the internal dialogues that repeat and reinforce these experiences in our lifetime. Much, perhaps most, of these data and emotions are fear-based. These experiences form the basis of a set of stories we create from collected data and emotions. Unfortunately, these stories do not contain all the data from these events and activities. Much of the actual data is either missed or lost. In any given event, it is impossible to consciously pay attention to everything around us. There is a recommendation in the "One Minute Manager" course by Kenneth Blanchard, Ph.D., that you rewrite your notes taken from a workshop within the first 24 hours or not more than 48 hours. Consider your short-term memory; if the current data is not saved to your long-term memory, you lose your ability to consciously retrieve that data. The data is not entirely lost; you just don't know where to find it. Have you ever tried to find a file that you could not remember how you named or saved it? It's not lost but it is difficult to find. So, when you revisit an event or activity in your mind, you don't have available to you the complete data set as well as the emotional content. "You are not playing with a full deck." Therefore, the story you create about any given event is skewed.

We all have our stories, and that's why we can't understand why people do what they do. Eckhart Tolle has a excellent quote in his book (page 113), Stillness Speaks,

"If her past were your past, her pain your pain, her level of consciousness your level of consciousness, you would think and act exactly as she does."

This quote says everything to me about stories. Native Americans have a similar saying that "you have to walk a mile in someone else's shoes in order to understand them."

The most important component of the Story Body is the "Critical Voice." This Critical Voice is the culprit that causes me the most difficulty and is the source of much of the emotional pain I've experienced over the past year. If I let it run freely, I get into all kinds of trouble because it rarely creates dialogues that are favorable to my well-being. It wants to explain and understand everything. However, it can only do so in the context of the story or stories it accesses from the Story Body.

As a result, it forms the basis of all the dialogues that consume me at any given time. These dialogues are fear based and are repeated over and over, and many times overwhelm my ability to stay in the moment. During the past year, it has been so bad that I have exploded or "lost it" three occasions during the past year. In other words, my efforts to explain or understand events over a period of time, overload my ability to stay in control and subsequently lead to the explosions. In order to overcome these episodes, I've had to use every technique available to me to keep me sane or intact. Sometimes, it took several days of continual clearing in order to maintain my focus.

The best medicine has been my work. When I'm in a classroom or in a coaching or counseling sessions, within moments my mind becomes clear. I am at peace, and I feel in control of everything. For example, before I started a class a couple of years ago, I had been suffering with symptoms of a cold. It was an up or down battle that had lasted for several weeks. However, after two hours of conducting the class, all the symptoms disappeared and were gone for good.

Although my most difficult times have occurred when I'm in my office, my most productive period for working on myself occurs when I'm driving. As previously stated in the Chapter on Perception/Perspectives, when I'm in my car, my programmed mind drives the car and my conscious mind takes care of me by focusing on the potential problems that might occur. Thus, I am free to be in the moment once I let go of trying to get to my destination. As a result, my inner mind is free to process emotional blocks, plan activities or be creative. So, I have used this time to clear or release emotional blocks.

The emotional blocks are cleared using one or a combination of the following procedures. First, I identify whatever emotional-based event or experience that I am continually reliving. Second, I then initiate a clearing session that is based on a process of connecting with my Story Body. Finally, I experience these emotions until I feel clear. Another method is emotion dumping, where I replace the emotional energy in my Story Body with more stable energy until the emotional energy is cleared. At the end of each session, I "wash" down my Story Body to dissolve any residual emotional debris until I feel cleared.

Third, once I feel cleared, I relive the event or experience, but this time I would reenact the event or experience in a way that benefits me or at least the way I would like to have experienced it the first time. And, fourth, I don't blame someone else for what they did. I don't want to give away my power or become a victim. I do want to know how I got hooked or triggered. Once I can determine how I got hooked or triggered then I not only resolve the situation, but relive it in a way that benefits me.

Sometimes, after going through a session I would have a day, week, or even several weeks of clarity. After a least one or two of these sessions, I felt like I had experienced what it may be like to experience enlightenment. However, I knew it wouldn't last. This pattern has been in place for the past year beginning in December 2010. It has been one of the most difficult years of my life.

Working through my Story Body episodes has allowed me to see some of the more difficult patterns that have been with me since I was a child. As a result, I can better accept me as I am, and

"Just Be Thomas." I recognize that I don't have to take care of people; I can see the triggers most of the time before they are fired off. And I've had a chance to release the patterns of misplaced focus, when you can't see the forest for the trees or the trees for the forest for that matter. I am still working to clear these patterns.

After spending this past year clearing my Story Body, I can better appreciate this past year as a growth year that has been preparing me for the rest of my life. For instance, I was profiled by a Taos policeman, last August in Taos, NM. I was sitting in front of a store in a business area. While sitting there, I saw a policeman walking down the walkway about 20 to 30 yards from me. As I looked at him and he looked at me, I felt a very strong emotional hit that I have not felt since I was a young man. I was immediately filled with fear and felt that I had done something wrong. I had forgotten what it was like to experience such a hit. I will include a report of this experience in the appendix section.

The emotional response I experienced with the policeman was later confirmed. He did identify me as a potential problem. However, I didn't allow that fear to overtake me; so, I was able to respond in an appropriate manner. If I had not had the three explosions during the previous eight months, I shudder to think what might have happened. I was able to maintain my composure, in spite of the triggered event and not lose it emotionally. I was able to be in the moment.

So, this past year has been geared toward the process of clearing of my Story Bodies. Although this process is not complete, I can now look back at those experiences without regret and see them as learning and growth experiences. The experience in Taos may have even been a graduation exercise and a window to the next level.

The books that come after this one will be based on not just the past year but will include the understanding and information generated during at least the past three years. I look forward to the writing and completion of this work.

A Proposed Theme for the Next Book

There are a lot of people who want to save the earth. I ask all who do, "Why does the earth need saving?" In my twenties and thirties, I wanted to change the world and put Blacks in control; until I realized that put Blacks in control would not change anything. I went through several permutations before I realized it wouldn't change the world. It would just put another group in charge.

After studying with various religious, psychological, and metaphysical groups, I realized that I only needed to save myself. That is, I had to change my way of thinking, my behavior, in other words, the way I lived my life. So, I set out to change me. This book is based on the evolution of these changes.

Some twenty to thirty years later, I read a book, "Ishmael" by Daniel Quinn. Reading this book cemented the idea that the source of many of our problem stems from the programming we have received from our civilized world. Now, I am not demonizing the civilized world because I no longer view the civilized world as a right or wrong, good or bad thing. These programs give us an opportunity to overcome obstacles that lead to growth, development, and understanding. As a result, we can make conscious deliberate choices about how we live our lives. For me, this is road to enlightenment.

We (Humans) need to understand that there have been at least five (some say six, seven, even ten) mass extinction during the life of the earth. The extinctions were the result of changes caused by natural events like volcanoes, global warming or cooling, as well as external events like the impacts of asteroids and meteors. Those species that could not live in the flow of these changes did not survive.

The first extinction may be of interest to humans (unificationtheory.com). The earth at that time was covered by anaerobic (without oxygen) bacteria. These bacteria as all living beings do, gave off a waste product. This waste product was oxygen. The bacteria gave off so much oxygen that the atmosphere of earth was changed from an anaerobic to an aerobic (without oxygen to oxygenated) environment. A large percentage of these bacteria disappeared. So, the extinction of these bacteria was directly related to their own waste product.

The civilized world is gradually taking over the earth, destroying forest, wildlife, and habitats. Some see this take over as being similar or like that of a virus. So, if we don't change, more than likely it will change for us and that might lead to our (human) extinction. The earth does not play; it can and will take care of itself. Therefore, we, humans, must change.

Appendices

Appendix I
Bibliography

Appendix II: The Holistic Warrior's Favorite Quotations and Affirmations

1. Do what you love and money will follow
2. Your path is created as you walk it
3. What power corrupts, poetry cleanses
4. Just be Thomas; and Persevere
5. He who knows not and knows that he knows not is a wise man. He who knows not and doesn't know that he knows not is a fool!
6. Ask and you shall receive
7. Law of Life: Give and Receive
8. When you have done your best, you might not win but you'll never lose
9. If her past were your past, her pain your pain, her level of consciousness your level of consciousness, you would think and act exactly as she does.
10. Be here now
11. Love is all there is
12. If you think you got it, you got it. If you don't think you got it, even if you got it, you don't got it
13. I Am embraces the present; I Am transforms the past; I Am lets go of the future
14. HO'OPONOPONO - 'I love you, I'm sorry, please forgive me, thank you, thank you, thank you
15. Money is a Living Entity. I want to connect with it and not see it in Fear or as an Enemy
16. You become what you resist – Patricia Sun
17. He who knows not and knows that he knows not is a wise man, but he who knows not and knows that he knows not is a Fool. – Melvin Tolson
18. You don't fail unless you quit.
19. There are no failures in communication, just outcomes – Blander and Grinder (NLP)
20. You don't know what you don't know. – Mary Baranski
21. Let go of the past and play the hand you were dealt. – In Plain Sight 5-11-12 episode

22. As we work to complete our goals, i.e., driving a car; we are constantly off course. In order to arrive at our designation safely, we automatically make thousands of corrections to stay on course and reach our goal. If we miss just one, we probably won't make our goal. – Adapted from Ken Blanchard's One Minute Manager's course.
23. The intention of all behaviors is positive. - Blander and Grinder (NLP)
24. The map is not the Territory. - Blander and Grinder (NLP)
25. The Law of Life: Give and Receive. If this law is not followed, then nothing and the earth itself or anywhere else can survive. So, it is not better to give than receive. It is better to give and receive; when you do so you can give unlimited because you will never get drained. – Nolan
26. Love can be expressed on many levels at once:
    a. LOVE   Creator
    b. Love   Connection with all things of creation
    c. love   connection between individuals
    d. luv   Attachment
    e. love and luv are on the same level

    Luv is based on attachment, control; one way and thus creates Win-Lose. Love is based on connection; both ways and thus creates Win-Win. – Nolan
27. Attachment is suffering, let gooooo! – Caption on a Tee-Shirt I bought in Colorado years ago.
28. Everybody has their own story (or Stories) that they created based on their perception of life. It not real because it never happened that way. It is also not right or wrong good or bad; it's yours, theirs, and mine. So, in any situation there is your version, their version, my version and what actually happened. - Nolan
29. Do not believe in something just because you heard it - Andrés Segovi
30. Your story may not have such a happy beginning
    but that doesn't make you who you are
    It is the rest of your story; who you choose to be
    So, who are you Panda? – The Soothsayer, Kung Fu Panda 2

The Holistic Warrior's Mantra

Observe

Allow

Let Go!!!

Appendix III: Aura Photos, Etc.

Aura Photo (A)

Aura Photo (B)

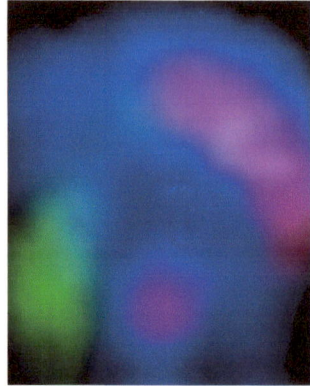

Aura Chakra Photo (C)

1. **Aura Photo (A)** - note the Six-Pointed Star over the heart area
2. **Aura Photo (B)** – look closely at the pink image bottom in the middle of the photo, it is surrounded by a blue Six-Pointed Star
3. **Aura Chakra Photo (C)** - note the clear and geometric chakra figures. Usually the chakra figures are irregular and in different colors

Holistic Warrior Poster Logo

Holistic Warrior Poster Logo; the three eagle figures represent three major Scorpion influences in my astrological chart

Holistic Warrior Crest Logo

Holistic Warrior Crest Logo; combining three aura photos with the Holistic Warrior Poster Logo
The Six-Pointed Star also shows up in the combined photos. Note the solid and dashed line six-pointed figure super-imposed over the photos.

Holistic Warrior's Book Cover*

*This Book Cover art work was created by Rick Ferguson of One Force Productions in Houston, TX. Note that the Six-Pointed Star can be configured in this image, as seen on the image on the next page.

The three eagle figures represent the triple Scorpion influences from my astrological chart. My Sun and Rising signs are in Scorpio. My Moon is in Leo. Since my Leo Moon conjuncts Pluto, I have a triple Scorpion influences. All three Scorpion signs are between 10 and 20 degrees, hence, the three eagles.

The three aura figures were taken from the three aura photos on page 198.

Holistic Warrior's Book Cover
With the Super-imposed Six-Pointed Star

Aura Chakra Photo

This image represents a different illustration of my aura; notice that my chakras are nearly balanced in this image, as well.

www.ingramcontent.com/pod-product-compliance
Lightning Source LLC
Chambersburg PA
CBHW040131270326
41929CB00001B/1